Architectural Timber Battens

Edgar (Ted) Stubbersfield

CONTENTS

ACKNOWLEDGMENTS

It is said that plagiarism is when you copy from one book and research is when you copy from two. Perhaps, but when looking at the subject of architectural timber battens I could not find even the first book from which to copy so I had to start from the beginning. I was greatly assisted by the following people:

Ralph Bailey
    Principal Architect, Guymer Bailey Architects
Dave Collinson,
    Technical Manager, Buildex ITW.
Holly Williams
    Feilden Clegg Bradley Studios
Geoff Dennis,
    Deputy Director, Property and Facilities Division, UQ.
John Grealy,
    Director, Architectus Brisbane
Mark Hogan
    Senior Designer, Architectus Brisbane.
Brian Hooper
    Principal, Brian Hooper Architects
David Johnston
    Senior Associate, Populous
Stephen Koch
    Business Development Manager, Arch Wood Protection
Philip Leeson
    Principal, Philip Leeson Architects.
Colin MacKenzie,
    Technical Consultant, Timber Queensland.

John Mainwaring
    Director, JMA Architects Qld Pty Ltd.
Roger Mainwood
    Principal Director, Total project Group
Jason Millard
    Contract Draftsman
Steve Napier
    Woodform
Mark Paroz
    Sales Representative, Vulcan Stainless.
Jessica Riske
    Practice Manager, Wilson Architects.
Embassy of the Kingdom of the Netherlands,
    Canberra
Ed Scott
    Timber consultant
Stadiums Queensland
Bill Thorn
    Parkside Timbers.
Rudy Uytenhaak
    Principal, Rudy Uytenhaak Architectenbureau

While this book does not claim to represent the views of the Department of Agriculture and Fisheries and the Forest Corporation of NSW, the assistance of three of their officers is especially acknowledged.

Martin Grealy
    Senior Manager, Marketing, Forest Corporation of NSW,

Gary Hopewell MSc
    Principal Scientist, Horticulture and Forestry Science, Agri-Science Queensland.

Jane Siebuhr
    Senior Project Officer Resources, Department of Agriculture and Fisheries.

INTRODUCTION

This small book started off as a request from Architectus, a prominent Brisbane architectural firm, to develop a continuing professional development seminar on the subject of architectural timber battens. There has been an increasing use of these battens in Queensland, and indeed Australia wide, over recent years and while they can certainly look excellent when first installed, they have the potential to be a maintenance nightmare. Following the failure of a high profile batten project where one fell to the ground, it needs to be recognised that there is the potential in a people occupied space for litigation.

When researching the subject I came to the conclusion that while these concerns were valid, they did not have to be the accepted consequence of using timber. If some basic steps are taken it will result in a long lived feature that ages well even in tropical and subtropical architecture. The following chapters will take you through the issues involved in designing to achieve that end. I could find no books on the subject so, without the generous help of those I have acknowledged, this design aid for professionals would not have been possible.

Most of the projects illustrated are from Queensland in Australia which the travel advertisements say is renowned for being "beautiful one day and perfect the next" (just another way of saying it is a harsh climate). Systems that work in the Queensland environment will perform better in cooler climates.

1. WHY USE TIMBER BATTENS

Australia was first settled by Europeans in 1788. With scarce resources, Great Britain being six months away by sailing ship and infrastructure for a whole nation having to be built on a very small budget, the very durable locally available hardwoods were the natural material for homes, bridges and commercial public buildings. Despite often being poorly maintained and poorly designed[1] many, indeed most of the structures, gave and some are still giving very satisfactory service. No other material but timber could do this and all this was achieved by workers with moderate skills and basic tools.

Particularly following World War Two, timber fell out of favour as a building material, being seen as yesterday's material. That view is slowly changing. The modern substitutes have now been in service for long enough for honest appraisals to be made of their performance. Fortunately for timber, its reputation as a structural[2] and aesthetic material is being restored. A leading Queensland architect put this succinctly saying, "Well-designed Timber components are rarely matched by other materials for their natural beauty and warmth that age gracefully with little maintenance if designed within the parameters of the species."[3]

Fig. 1. Federation style home using timber for architectural enhancement.

Fig. 2. Vertical battens used as a decorative skirt and on second row of posts to enclose under Queenslander style house.

Timber is now going through a renaissance. Shortly before starting this book I finalised a chapter for the French publication, *Le Mémento du Forestier* which dealt with timber construction. That chapter was to contain a section on modern highly processed timber in its various forms but the editors decided

---

[1] In Queensland, timber highway bridges are still being reconstructed against plans drawn in 1936 despite the understanding of timber design having advanced dramatically since that time.

[2] Road bridges in concrete and steel in the USA have been downgraded from 100 to 50 years while timber bridges have been upgraded from 50 to 75 years. With extra attention the timber bridge can now be certified for 100 years!

[3] Grealy, John. *Pers. Com.* May 14, 2015. Note the emphasis on species which will be explored through this book

against including that. It was felt that whatever was written would very quickly be out of date.

So while we are headed into uncharted waters with structural members, architectural battens have not gone away completely. They hark back to the very best of our heritage. From colonial days it was common sense even for a basic worker's cottage to have a window shade incorporating timber to protect from the extremes of weather we could experience. Perpendicular timber battens often enclosed under houses built on timber stumps.

A noticeable trend in modern Australian architecture has been the rediscovery of the advantages of timber battens. But no longer just for the practicality of shading the windows or enclosing under houses, but going far beyond to bestowing the overall character of the structure. Just as the home in Figure One used timber to give life to brick, in the same way timber is being used successfully to give a soul to a stark but otherwise functional concrete, glass and steel building.

Fig. 3. Forty-six kilometres of recycled battens were used on the outside of Lang Park stadium in Brisbane and give the structure its distinctive Australian flavor.

But designers need not look to tradition to find inspiration for the use of timber battens. The stadium at Lang Park (Figure Three) demonstrates that battens can stand as a contemporary medium in their own right and can look appropriate. They are attractive and can be low maintenance while, at the same time, being one of the most environmentally responsible products it is possible to use. But to balance the positives, and there are many, we must also accept the reality that, despite the improved aesthetics, "They are an ongoing nightmare!"[4] or at very least have the potential to be. As you read through this book, I trust you will see that timber is no different to steel or concrete, that there are certain things that you do, or don't do, at your peril. In exactly the same way, if you accommodate and work with the limitations, the medium you are designing with rewards you and your client. Successive chapters will guide you through the peculiarities of timber, and more specifically, Australian hardwood.

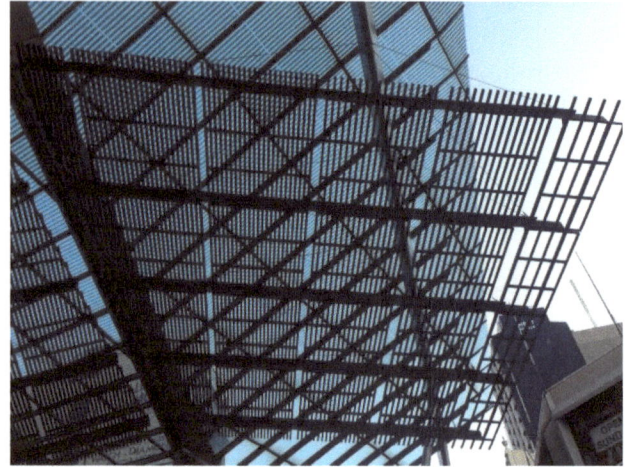

Fig. 4. Shade structures in Queen Street Mall as originally constructed with timber battens.

Fig. 5. Timber was replaced with aluminium which no longer plays with light.

Tradition combined with modernity are good reasons for using timber battens architecturally but another reason a designer might choose timber over other materials is the way it plays with light. Some extraordinary shade structures were built in the Queen Street Mall in Brisbane around the year 2000. Unfortunately, timber battens fastened underneath the frame were not a success and were replaced with aluminium.[5] An architect commented about the replacement battens, "As you walk up Albert Street from King George Square they appear as a solid black sheet whereas before, with the timber, you could

---

[4] Mainwaring, John. *Pers. Com.* April 27, 2015.

[5] The reason for this failure will be discussed in the chapter *Details of Design* under the section Safety in Design.

always see the light pattern coming through".[6]   The battens on Lang Park (Figure Three) also are intended to play with light and this was achieved by tapering the bottom as well as the top of the timber.[7]

Fig. 6. Project: AIIM Microscopy, Wollongong
Architect: Jacobs   **Material:** Vitex, Spotted Gum

Fig. 7. Project: Dutch Embassy, Canberra
Architect: Rudy Uytenhaak (Netherlands) Philip Leeson Architects (Australia)
Material: Spotted Gum

As I looked at the subject, it was difficult determine when a batten could cease to be a called a batten and became a cladding. A good example is the striking way that the architects of the Dutch Embassy in Canberra (Figure Seven) used a proprietary batten system giving it the visual effect of a cladding. The whole subject challenges traditional definitions of what a batten is.[8] The approach of this book will be to avoid discussing cladding completely and consider an architectural timber batten to be any regular spaced timbers used in part for decorative effect either internally or externally. This guide will include projects where larger size timbers have been used, such as the 'Tree of Knowledge' in Barcaldine (refer to its case history in the final chapter).

---

[6] Mainwaring, John. *Pers. Com*. April 27, 2015.
[7] Refer also to the Case History, University of Queensland, Ipswich Campus, Activity Centre.
[8] A batten has been defined as "any sawn timber section with cross-section dimensions of less than 25 mm thick and 25 mm – 50 mm wide or in timber classification, a sawn softwood section with cross-section dimensions of 44 mm – 100 mm thick and 100 mm – 200 mm wide, always considerably wider than thicker". Davies, Nikolas, Erkki Jokiniemi, *Dictionary of Architecture and Building Construction*. (Oxford: Architectural Press, 2008) 34.

Fig. 8. Tree of Knowledge, Barcaldine. **Architect:** Brian Hooper Architects. **Material:** Recycled power poles

2. INTERNAL BATTENS

The internal use of timber battens is far simpler than when they are installed externally. When used externally a designer has to consider:

- species selection,
- preservation of sapwood,
- grade quality,
- good air circulation,
- water shedding profile,
- suitable fasteners to avoid corrosion and
- coatings and maintenance versus natural weathering to grey.

These factors will be considered in detail in following chapters where we will see their importance but for all practical purposes they have little impact on internal use.

Fig. 9. Queensland Industrial Relations Commission. **Architect:** Architectus Brisbane. **Material:** Tallowwood

When used internally there is no rain and less UV so the timber is far less stressed and coatings last far longer. There is no leaching of tannins to consider nor corrosion of fasteners. Because of their simplicity they can be dealt with briefly. But saying that they are simpler is not the same as saying it is trouble free. An experienced timber consultant spoke of one project saying:

> "One job I inspected several years ago involved an internal ceiling in an air conditioned building where the boards were fixed on edge in parallel for architectural effect. Unfortunately, the architect involved did not specify seasoned timber and the fixing method was incorrect. You can imagine what happened.[9] Of course the architect and the builder tried to blame the timber."

The main considerations would be whether the timber is seasoned, its fire resistance should large quantities be used, and its colour. With Australian hardwoods it is impossible to dry commercially beyond 50 mm thick. So a product processed from say a 75x50 mm or 150x50 mm can be supplied kiln dried but remember you will need at least a three month lead time. This needs to be written into the project documentation. A product processed from say a 75x75 mm could not be supplied kiln dried and air drying for internal use will take three years.[10] So the practicality of kiln drying is going to influence the size of the batten you use.

Before specifying a size, it is important to check availability of the exact finished size you are considering as some designers forget to factor in shrinkage. Standard dressed green off saw hardwood is 5 mm under the nominal size, e.g. 75 mm dresses down to 70 mm. But kiln dried sizes are far more complicated and are calculated as follows:

Take the standard nominal sawn size as your starting point e.g. 75 mm
Deduct 3 mm sawing tolerance 75-3 = 72 mm
Deduct shrinkage appropriate for the species e.g. 6% for spotted gum 72 – 4.3 = 67.7 mm
Allow dressing say 2.0-2.5 mm = 67.7 – 2.5 = 65 mm kiln dried size

This then gets complicated as a limited number of mills cut oversize which allows them to supply a finished kiln dried product at the same size as the green size. Unfortunately these mills generally only produce kiln dried product in a limited range of species. Spotted gum is more common in Queensland while blackbutt is more common in New South Wales but these species may not align with your species (i.e. colour) intensions. There is no hard and fast rule as to the best approach but it has to be considered and resolved before specifying and detailing something that cannot be supplied economically as it has to be produced from a larger size. Most mills will not fractional cut i.e. produce outside of Australian standard sizes, so while a 65 mm ironbark may be available it probably may not be available in 70 mm.

---

[9] If you can't imagine, there would have been gaps, twisting and bending.
[10] Hopewell, Gary. *Pers. Com*. April 24, 2015. "A rule-of-thumb for green hardwood used to be 1 year per 25 mm thickness, to 12%".

Species	Percentage of hardwood sawlog harvested from Qld State forests[11]	Percentage of hardwood sawlog harvested from NSW State forests[12]	Fire resistance AS 3959-2009	Lyctus susceptible
Spotted gum	68.81%	5.9%	Yes	Yes
Broad-leaved red ironbark	7.02%	2.01% Includes grey, mugga and broadleaf ironbark which are not resistant	Yes	No
Narrow-leaved red ironbark	4.60%		Yes	No
Blackbutt (not New England)	4.58%	15.84%	Yes	No
Silvertop Ash	NSW/Vic/Tas	0.12%	Yes	No
River red gum	Not common in Qld	5.41%	Yes	Yes
Turpentine	0.11%	0.25%	Yes	No
Kwila	Imported		Yes	Yes
Table 1. Fire resistant timbers, availability and lyctus susceptibility.				

In Table One, I have given the fire resistant species as listed in AS 3959-2009 and tabled their availability from managed Queensland and New South Wales state forests. Kwila/merbau, an imported hardwood, is readily available but designers should be aware of environmental concerns about logging practices.[13] Should fire resistance not be a consideration you have a wider choice which includes tallowwood and brush box. In that instance kiln dried cypress is also a reasonable species to consider.

The colour of Australian hardwoods varies considerably species from species and even within a species. A choice of white(ish), red and brown is available in the fire resistant species. Despite this variation the colour indicators in Figures Ten to Thirteen below are still a useful guide. But do not hold too great an expectation that the one metre sample supplied will be totally representative of the 10,000 metres ordered.

---

[11] Based on figures 2003 to 2013 from state forests and grazing leases and not expected to change in the short term. Seibuhr, Jane. *Pers. Com.* 12 Feb, 2015.

[12] Based on 2013-4 financial year and expected to be constant for 10 years. Grealy, Martin. *Pers. Com.* 13 July, 2015.

[13] In 2013, while visiting Indonesia, I met with someone from their government. He told of a national park where one million trees had been harvested illegally! I am getting sceptical in my old age and suspect it would all have been sold with a certificate and purchased in good faith! In this case, the offenders were caught and much of the timber was cut into short lengths and left to rot on the forest floor.

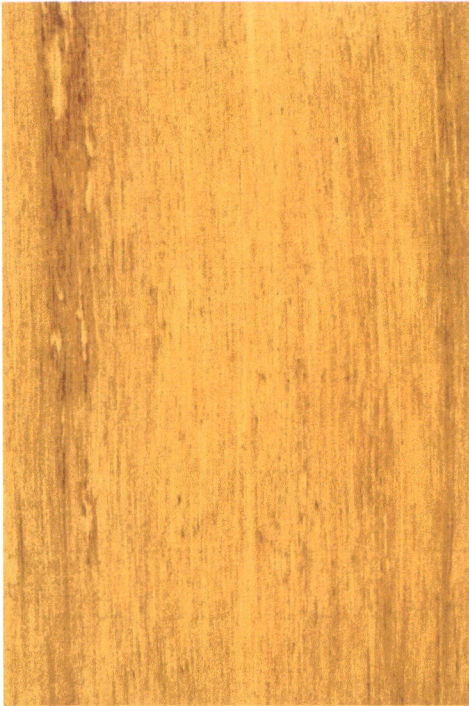

Fig. 10. Silvertop ash.

Fig. 11. Blackbutt.

Fig. 12. Spotted gum.

Fig. 13. River red gum.

The corrosion resistance of the fasteners for internal battens is straight forward. Even though there is no moisture, (the requirement for corrosion to occur), it is never good practice to use the zinc/yellow screws (refer Table Six). Choose instead either galvanized or stainless fixings as these can be relied on to perform well internally.[14] Treatment options are also more varied as it is only an H2 (Inside above ground) application. This means that decay is not an issue if it stays dry and treatment is only necessary if the timber is lyctus susceptible, (spotted gum, river red gum and kwila/merbau from Table One). You have the additional options of using boron or light organic solvent preservative (LOSP) internally on kiln dried hardwood. These two treatments are clear.[15] Boron is probably the better choice as it can be done prior to kiln drying whereas the LOSP treatment must be done after drying giving an opportunity for it to be missed. The LOSP treatment can also interfere with the finish being applied if it is not weathered for a period.

We will see that using external battens can be far more complex.

---

[14] Refer to my *Timber Preservation Guide* for a discussion of corrosion of fasteners.
[15] Refer to my *Timber Preservation Guide* for more information on the colour of preservatives.

3. TIMBER FOR EXTERNAL BATTENS

Imagine you have engaged an engineer to design a steel footbridge for you. On studying the plans you see that he/she had asked for steel, so badly rusted it had less than 50% of its original strength and there is no corrosion protection used. Would you build that bridge? Of course not, it is nonsense. My question then is, "Why do we do exactly the same thing with timber, because this is what we do when we order timber by F rating, and then complain when it fails"?[16] It could have done nothing else! That you achieved any sort of life at all is a testimony to the material, not a criticism

Fig. 14. The F14 equivalent of steel.

It is generally not understood that when specifying/ordering timber only by an F grade, that it says nothing meaningful about the properties of external decorative timber. When we say F14, what we are asking for is a grade of timber where the basic working stress in bending is approximately 14 megapascals (MPa). And that is on the day it was milled, not after twenty years being fully exposed to the weather! Table Two shows the values for F14 at the time the stress grading was introduced.[17] It says not one word about the properties that are critical which are durability, stability, shrinkage and inadequately deals with appearance. But when you combine it with a joint group these values make it possible to design roof trusses which never see the light of day or any moisture. An F rating alone does not allow you to design architectural battens but can engender a false sense of security about the specification.

Stress Grade	Type of Stress				Modulus of Elasticity
	Bending	Tension parallel to grain	Shear in Bending	Compression parallel to grain	
F14	14.0	11.0	1.25	10.5	12500
Table 2. Basic Working Stresses and Modulus of Elasticity (MPa).[18]					

Far more attention has to be given to the design of external timber battens than roof trusses. This chapter will look at the first three of the critical considerations mentioned in the previous chapter:

- species selection,
- preservation of sapwood and
- grade quality.

---

[16] Refer to my book *Grading Hardwood* where this is explained in detail.

[17] Despite the move away from working stress to limit state engineering, the F designations were retained as they were convenient.

[18] Kloot, H. *The Strength Group and Stress Grade Systems* in CSIRO Forest Products Newsletter No 394 (Sept-Oct 1973) (CSIRO: South Melbourne 1973). 3.

Species Selection

There are over 200 species of hardwood milled commercially in Australia. Their properties vary dramatically. Some are suitable only for making disposable pallets and dunnage while a very few are among the best hardwoods in the world. Some species have very high shrinkage e.g. turpentine but are very durable and stable when kiln dried but only harvested in small quantities. Again turpentine which would be a very good batten comprises only one tenth of one percent of Queensland's production and only a quarter of a percent from New South Wales. Fortunately, some of the best timbers for architectural battens are among the most commonly harvested at least in Queensland and sufficiently common in New South Wales.

Species	% of sawlog from Qld State forests	% of sawlog from NSW State forests	Royal species	Durability above ground	pH class[19]
Spotted gum	68.81%	5.90%	Yes	1	2
Broad-leaved red ironbark	7.02%	2.01% Ironbarks not separated in NSW reports	Yes	1	3
Narrow-leaved red ironbark	4.60%		Yes	1	3
Grey ironbark	4.45%		Yes	1	3
Tallowwood	0.92%	1.27%	Yes	1	3
Gympie messmate	1.23%	0	Yes	1	3
Forest red gum	2.66%	.01%	No	1	2
Grey box	1.57%	0.08%	Yes	1	3
White mahogany	1.42%	.047%	No	1	3
Grey gum	0.61%	0.30%	Yes	1	3
Red mahogany	0.43%	0.40%	No	1	3
Kwila/Merbau	Imported		N/A	1	2

Table 3. Availability, royal species, durability and pH class.

So how does the uninitiated know what are the very best species to use? There was a simple term that was used when durable timber was required. It would be ordered as "royal species". This has been defined as "A collection of eucalypt timbers which command a premium in price because of their great

---

[19] Nguyen, Minh N, Robert H. Leicester, and Chi-hsiang Wang. *Embedded Corrosion of Fasteners in Exposed Timber Structures* (Forest and Wood Products Association: Melbourne 2008) 19-20.

durability and strength".[20] But what constitutes this collection? I have met people who claim to have a seen a definitive list but no one has been able to point me to a document where it can actually be found.[21] Until I can find such a list, the prevailing and probably correct view is that this was a marketing term adopted by the industry. An old (90 years plus) senior forester recalled it this way - to be a royal species the timber had to be:

- Highly durable
- readily available
- extractable and
- have a ready market.

The significance of the last three points is that the timber was not a "boutique" or "craft" species that is not available in large enough quantities to be commercial. For structural timber, royal species included grey and red ironbark, spotted gum (above ground applications), tallowwood and yellow stringybark. The list varied from state to state and in Western Australia included jarrah and karri despite being of lower durability than the eastern Australian list.[22]

Unfortunately, on searching for this term on the internet, I found some mills in New South Wales advertising very inappropriate species as being "royal". So a very useful description has been devalued and effectively lost. You cannot go wrong with the old forester's list as far as durability is concerned. You can go wrong when you then insist on a species that has low availability.[23] You can go wrong also when you choose a species on colour and not on durability. My preference would be for spotted gum because of its ready availability and natural oils. Notwithstanding confusion over the term, I will still use the "royal species" term through this book.

Preservation

The sapwood of all species is rated as In Ground and Above Ground Durability Class 4. This means that the sapwood of ironbark is rated as the same durability as the sapwood of pine. Preservation of the sapwood was optional for non lyctus susceptible species when used internally because of the lack of moisture but it is essential for all species, lyctus susceptible or not, when used externally. But note that I

---

[20] Anonymous. *Dictionary of Timber Terms* (Timber Secretarial Group: Sydney U.D.) 12.

[21] The closest I have come to a list is found in the Road and Traffic Authority report *Timber truss road bridges - A strategic approach to conservation, July 2011* where it says on Page 16 "These bridges need 'royal' species (Grey Box, Ironbark, Tallowwood and Grey Gum) as used in the original designs. Lesser timbers such as Blackbutt or Spotted Gum are inferior, have less strength and deteriorate at a faster rate, thus requiring more frequent replacement" (New South Wales Government, July 2011). The report can be found at http://www.rms.nsw.gov.au/documents/projects/key-build-programs/maintenance/timber-truss-road-bridges/timber-truss-road-bridges-report-july11.pdf. Spotted gum would be a sought out species for bridge work in Queensland but this may well reflect the variability between fast and slow grown timber.

[22] Smith, Walter. *Pers. Com.* Jan 18, 2013.

[23] We quoted a large quantity of tallowwood architectural battens shortly before writing this book. This species makes up less than 1% of the Queensland forestry harvest but it is more common in NSW. We found one NSW mill that may have been able to supply at the future time required and another that could guarantee supply. There was 20% difference in price between definite and maybe. If costed on a possibility it may have caused major problems at the time of supply.

said preservation of sapwood, not the timber.

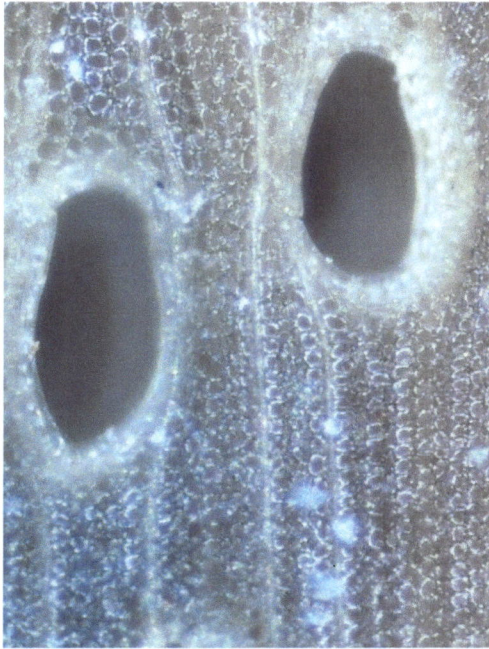

Fig 15. Empty sapwood vessels.   Fig 16. Closed heartwood vessels.

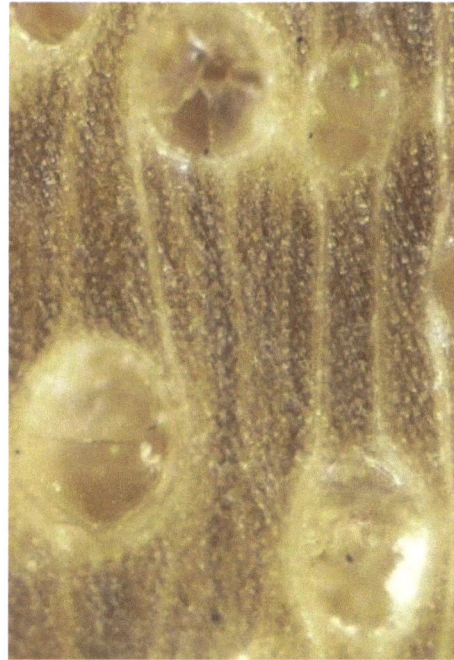

Figures Fifteen and Sixteen show the sapwood and heartwood (also called truewood) of tallowwood. It is evident that the vessels in the sapwood are porous allowing the treatment chemicals to flow through them. By contrast the vessels in the heartwood are plugged. These occlusions are called tyloses. **Timber preservation only works on sapwood**. It has absolutely no effect on the heartwood whether pine or hardwood. The old adage states that "You cannot make a silk purse out of a sow's ear". And in like manner you cannot raise the performance of the heartwood of non royal sawn timber such as blackbutt through preservation. You can only stabilise the sapwood. Preservation must be viewed, not as the primary means of achieving durability but as an enhancement of timber with already naturally high durability.

The application is H3, (external above ground) so it gives you a number of options for the type of preservation. These are:

- waterborne
    - CCA
    - ACQ
    - Tanalith E
- solventborne
    - LOSP

There are restrictions on the use of CCA imposed by the Australian Pesticides and Veterinary Medicines Authority (APVMA)[24] but architectural battens is not a restricted use so it is possible to receive CCA treated battens if care is not taken. As well there is some concern in the industry about the effectiveness of LOSP used externally. You need to specify either:

VPI[25] treated to H3 with ACQ or Tanalith E, CCA and LOSP not permitted or
VPI treated to H4 with ACQ or Tanalith E, CCA not permitted.

If I was producing the battens I would use the first specification. An architect that does not have the control I have might specify the second option as a further guarantee not to receive LOSP treated timber. Can the timber be purchased without sapwood? Perhaps for smaller quantities but with great difficulty and much added expense. My personal philosophy is that ordering sap free is a **very irresponsible** use of a limited resource and any environmental credits claimed should be forfeited.

Fig. 17. Timber dressed after (LH) and prior (RH) to treating.

The treatment will affect the colour of the timber. If treated as a pack of rough sawn timber prior to any processing, Tanalith E and ACQ will turn every face a uniform brown colour. If you were just using a rough sawn batten it would not matter which of the royal species you used or even a mixture thereof. The shrinkage and the durability are very similar. When writing your specification, do not write in difficulties that do not need to be there such as insisting on a single species when the treatment process will hide its natural colour.

Should you require a dressed finish from the same treated timber, the sapwood will have turned a brown colour. However, it is of little consideration because it will not be very noticeable up close and completely lost when installed. By dressing after treating, the natural colour of the timber will be

---

[24] Any product claiming to be a preservative has to have its evidence verified by the APVMA. Note references to Lanolin being a preservative in the chapter Leaching and Finishing.
[25] VPI is an abbreviation for vacuum pressure impregnation.

restored and then it is usual to have single species. Sometimes the option is chosen to process the timber and then to treat giving a uniform brown colour again. A species mix is then acceptable. This is the best option as far as disposing of shavings produced in the dressing process.

There is no right or wrong answer as it is a matter of choice and in the long run does not matter a great deal as the battens will all go a uniform silver grey if nothing is done to the timber. For a more complete discussion on preservation refer to my *Timber Preservation Guide*.

Grade Quality
Grading new timber

Even a piece of royal species spotted gum might only be fit for use in a packing case if the grade is not correct. By "grade" (without the F in front of it), the timber industry refers to the amount of natural feature that the piece contains. Natural feature is a euphemism for **defect**. There are four recognised Structural Grades described in both AS 2082 Timber - Hardwood - Visually stress-graded for structural purposes and AS2858 Timber—Softwood—Visually stress-graded for structural purposes. The F ratings are based on matching the Strength Group[26] of a species with one of the four Structural Grades in AS2082 and AS 2858. These are applied in exactly the same way for unseasoned and seasoned product. The Structural Grades are meant to represent a percentage of the strength of timber when free of any natural feature. Those percentages are found in Table Four - note how low the percentage is for some Structural Grades. What makes the difference in the percentage is the size of the defects such as knots, that each of the grades allow.

When produced from the timbers of South East Queensland, these lower F grades are visually unacceptable. Yet we see some professional designers, who just see a number with an F in front of it, asking for grades that are far lower than 38% of the strength of solid timber[27]. Visually and structurally they are appalling.

Structural Grade:	% of clear wood strength
No. 1	75%
No. 2	60%
No. 3	48%
No. 4	38%

Table 4. Structural Grades as a percentage of solid wood.

Species	Unseasoned	Seasoned
Tallowwood	F22	F27
Spotted gum	F17	F27
Sydney blue gum	F14	F22
Jarrah	F11	F17

Table 5. Different grades produced from Structural Grade 2 hardwood.

Also what is not appreciated is how variable the timber can be if just ordered as say F17. In unseasoned spotted gum that is Structural Grade 2. But that same level of defect in a piece of timber can produce anywhere from F27 to F11 depending on the species and whether it is kiln dried or not. (Refer to Table Five).

---

[26] Each species, including both pine and hardwood fits into one of seven strength groups for unseasoned and eight for seasoned timber.

[27] Refer to my comments on F14 and F17 KD specification in my *Grading Hardwood* guide.

When specifying your batten timber it is important to document away from AS 2082. The top and weather side should be graded to Structural Grade One; the back and bottom should be graded to a minimum of Structural Grade 2. This is irrespective of species. How does this equate to an F grade for the engineer? For hardwood, use the strength group of the species (for a range of species use the lowest group) and assume Structural Grade 2 and then use AS2082 to give you an F grade. But very importantly, the engineer's documentation and the architects must say the same thing. Frequently, they do not. I would not have an F grade on either professional's documentation; just the structural grades of the faces. If one professional has a higher grade than the other, you can expect the lower grade will be supplied by the tenderer with the lowest price.

From experience, I have found that some contractors have to be forced into doing the right thing, and the right thing in this case is to install the timber with the **best faces aligned correctly**. I achieved this by either making products that were not reversible or by branding the timber with a stamp or a staple on waterproof label as to the faces that should be aligned away from view.

Grading Recycled Timber
There are two interim standards for recycled timber. These are PN06.1039 Structural Recycled and PN06:1039 Decorative Recycled (yes, the numbers are the same). Though the effect of the batten is largely decorative, we can dismiss the decorative standard as the timber has to perform like a piece of structural timber. Whereas the standards for visually grading sawn hardwood and pine recognize four different grades, the structural standard only recognizes two grades - Recycled Grade 1 and Recycled Grade 2. The better grade, Recycled Grade 1, is basically the same as Structural Grade 2 in AS2082 (or 60% of the strength of defect free timber). This is too low a grade for external battens and cannot give you the required high quality weather resisting face and edge. This is particularly the case with smaller pieces.

You must resist the pressure that will be exerted from the recycled industry to revert to the interim recycled standard. It is in their interests, not yours. Architectural battens are not an oversized feature piece for people to look at and ponder the history. They have to perform on minimum size.

Other Related Matters

Unseasoned or Kiln Dried
The practicalities of kiln drying were discussed under the subject of Internal Battens. While critical for internal battens there is more leeway when they are used externally. Large sizes simply cannot be dried but small sizes can be, The very large amount of battens on Lang Park (refer to the case history) could only be classed as semi dried and generally they are working. As a general rule I believe you should aim for kiln drying of sawmill recovery sizes as this is relatively easy but you could accept a higher moisture content of say up to 18%. Larger sizes such as 150x50 mm I would be hesitant to dry simply because the logistics.

Confirmation grading
Grading from different producers can vary dramatically. Too often I have seen reliable and responsible suppliers lose orders on price, only to find that the lower price came at ignoring specifications.[28] Part of your documentation should include the requirement of third party confirmation grading of the timber. This can be arranged through Timber Queensland and others.

---

[28] Refer to the case histories in my book, *Grading Hardwood*.

Timber pH
The importance of the pH of the timber selected, as listed in Table Three, will be discussed in the chapter Details of Design. This can have an impact on fasteners and support system.

What is the Best Size Batten?
When considering the size of your batten you should be aware of what are known in the sawmilling industry as "recovery sizes". There include 50x25 mm, 50x38 mm, 38x38 mm and 50x50 mm. These recovery sizes are what can be cut from the remainder of the flitch after the main structural size has been sawn. Normally these smaller sizes are not sawn at all and the piece simply goes down the chipper. One miller stated that they were "hardly worth producing as the cost of stripping and drying usually outweighs the return. Most companies just buy the wider boards and rip them to obtain what they require in those sizes".[29] The case history, University of Queensland, Ipswich, Student Activity Centre shows a creative use of recovery sizes.

Cutting wider boards into smaller ones seems a poor use of resource. With the definition of recycled timber being so vague, and if timber that was destined for the chipper is diverted into product, it deserves to be eligible for green points. It certainly entitles you, legitimately, to that very nebulous "warm fuzzy feeling" and do not discount that as it is important to many customers. To obtain recovery sizes it is simply a matter of making arrangements beforehand with the miller and being prepared to pay a fair price for the material. If you are using recovery sizes then it is important that your documentation nominate where the timber can be purchased and to stipulate that the contractor is to provide proof that the timber has been ordered three months before the required date and to the stipulated grade. Experience has shown that some contractors will win the tender on the price provided by the nominated supplier and then shop around many suppliers to find lower priced material of the same size. There is a danger that the specification is lost and/or the timber is not ordered in time.

Should the planned batten be outside the recovery size then width to thickness may become an issue if you plan to align the battens horizontally. My experience with decking, another horizontal application, is that when going beyond **a ratio of 3.5:1** there is a danger of cupping. Acceptable sizes within this ratio are 150x50 mm and 120x35 mm and sizes outside are 150x38 mm and 200x50 mm. If the timber cups it holds moisture and deteriorates faster. Aligning vertically, that is in the horizontal axis but with the wider face against the support, avoids any issue that may result from cupping.

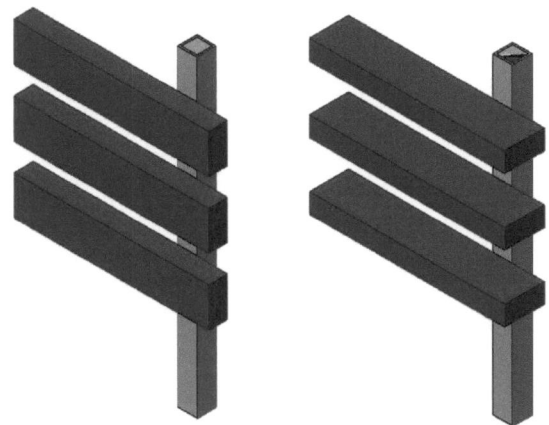

Fig. 18. Vertical and horizontal alignments of horizontally aligned battens

---

[29] Thorn, Bill. Sales Manager, Parkside Timbers. *Pers. Com.* May 7, 2015.

4. DETAILS OF DESIGN

The main thrust of this book is with horizontal battens as they are more challenging to design with and be successful than when they are aligned perpendicular. Put a bevelled top on a perpendicular batten and moisture shedding is complete. Keeping timber dry is the key to maximising life. Any successful weather exposed timber project is a combination of utilising the strengths of timber while at the same time accommodating its weaknesses which the perpendicular batten does best.

Correct species selection, while important is not the beginning and end of good design. Even high durability timbers will fail prematurely if you do not get the details of the design correct. This chapter will look at:

- good air circulation
- water shedding profile
- suitable fasteners to avoid corrosion and
- other related matters.

Fig. 19. No end clearance.

Fig. 20. Significant end clearance.

Air Circulation

For the longevity of the batten, your design needs to allow for good air circulation. You will have to consider clearances behind the batten, between each batten and at the ends of the batten. If you were building a boardwalk you would require a minimum of 200 mm between the timber and the ground because of the moisture present and lack of airflow. But when installed above ground, sustained moisture and high humidity are no longer a consideration. One proprietary system uses an aluminium channel to mount their battens. These channels are available in two thicknesses, 25 and 50 mm[30]. Colin Mackenzie, Technical Consultant to Timber Queensland recommends 35 mm minimum when there is good clearance between the battens.[31] The more clearance you can achieve the greater your chance of success. You will also need more clearance in the tropics than in Melbourne because of the humidity. It

---

[30] Woodform Architectural *Concept Click Batten Screening*. No publication details available, 8.
[31] Mackenzie, Colin. *Pers. Com.* April 25, 2015.

would seem reasonable to aim for 50 mm as the minimum back clearance for a design that suits all climatic conditions and get more if you can. I stress that this is for the batten health, not the building's. To achieve shading of the building a much bigger gap is needed. Refer to the case history on the Netherlands Embassy.

As for clearance between the battens themselves, they should function well with as little as 25 mm. I say this as I have had packs of rose gum air drying for almost twenty years with this amount of separation. There was no deterioration. Rose Gum is a Durability 2 Above Ground timber, well below that of the species I am recommending. But if you have the timber that close together it is more a cladding than a batten so you would expect your design to have spaces significantly more than that. That will, in turn, allow more airflow into the back.

The end gap needs to be a minimum of 6 mm. Any less than this and moisture can be held between the two ends by capillary action. Moisture enters end grain up to eight times faster than it does through the face so this gap is very important. This is where decay can be expected This gap can be difficult to achieve when you are trying to keep the end clearance of the screw from the end of the batten. Say you use a 14 gauge screw, which would be normal, and by the time you have eight diameters clearance that is 50 mm. So, by the time you add two times 50 mm, then 6 mm clearance then allow the screw to be say 10 mm from the edge of the steel, you need a frame that is 125 mm wide. It is probably better to allow for two narrower, less intrusive supports to achieve this than one very wide one.

Water Shedding Profile

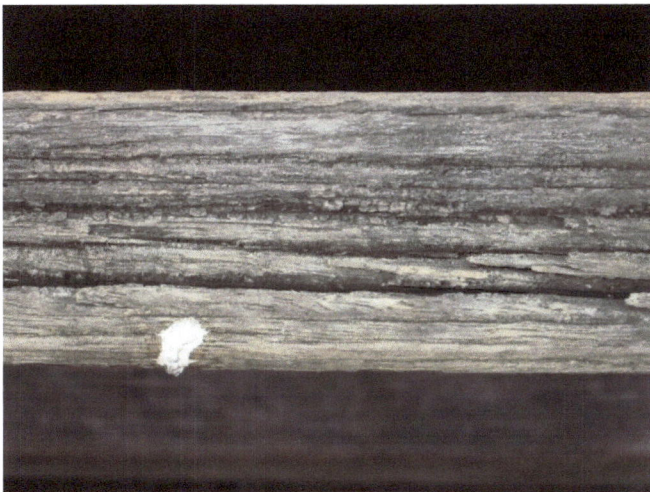

Fig. 21. Top of a 20 year old handrail.

Fig. 22. Top of a 30 year old crossarm.

When timber is installed with a flat top surface exposed to the weather, that surface will degrade much faster than if the surface is profiled or aligned to shed moisture. Figures Twenty-one and Twenty-two show royal species hardwood in two applications that have flat surfaces without any paint applied. The time period is twenty and thirty years respectively and the location for both was in the Lockyer Valley in Queensland, not a particularly aggressive environment. These images show vividly that a moisture shedding profile is absolutely vital to the long term success of an external timber batten.

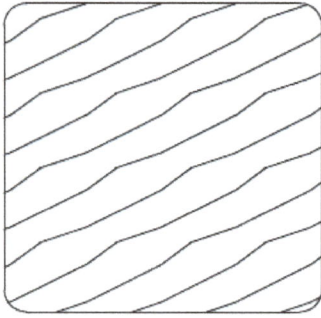

Standard Profile   Moisture Shedding Profiles

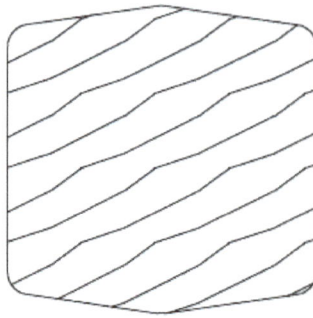

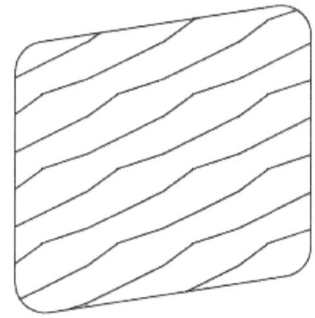

Fig. 23. Different batten profiles.

The normal way that a moisture shedding profile is achieved is by machining to a profile and two alternate designs are shown in Figure Twenty-three. Unquestionably, these will shed moisture and very importantly they are reversible allowing the correct alignment of best and worst faces. But these are probably not the ideal profile, at least for square sections.

Fig. 24. Fence at University of Queensland, Gatton Campus cricket ground 2014.

Fig. 25. Same fence in 1940.

The profile that has proven the most successful over a long period in Australia's climate has been a square set on edge. Just how successful can be seen in Figures Twenty-four and Twenty-five. The heritage listed fence at The University of Queensland's Gatton Campus was replaced in 2014. The same fence can be seen in the image taken in 1940. The fence probably should have been replaced ten years previously so this gives an effective service life of something like 65 years from the time the photograph was taken. There are no records as to when the fence was actually built. It would seem that, with selecting the right species and grade then taking care in how the timber is attached to the frame and the correct fastener is used, there is no reason why a 50 year life, even in Queensland, could not be achieved with the diamond configuration.

Dressed or Rough Sawn?

Consideration must be given to the surface texture. Thoughts automatically run to dressed profiles as they look better when first installed and, as they are an even size, they are easier to design and construct. But standard practice should be questioned and evaluated before being accepted. It is recognized that rough sawn timber performs much better than dressed in fully weather exposed applications.[32] The advantages of the dressed product can be kept by thicknessing the back and underside. This uniformity allows you to pencil round the corners as well in a single pass through the planer. If you choose a rough sawn thicknessed profile, specify that there are to be no toothed feed wheel marks on the exposed surface.

There can be a tradeoff between better initial aesthetics and longer life with lower maintenance with better aesthetics at the end of the life.

Suitable Fasteners

Screw durability was specified under AS 3566 Screws - Self-drilling - For the building and construction industries, which was introduced in 1988 in an attempt to counter the poor performance of imported fasteners particularly. Previously, compliance was to a material specification where products were deemed to comply if they had a certain coating thickness. The new standard adopted a stringent performance specification based on real life testing. For example, the test site for coastal use has to be "located less than 500 m from the mean high water line, in a coastal area with surf for most of the year".[33] Unfortunately this standard was withdrawn in 2015 though at the time of writing most suppliers are voluntarily complying with it. But the brand of screws allowed needs to be given more thought than before.[34] The Standard had four classes of corrosion resistance:

Class 1	For general internal use where corrosion resistance is of minor importance. Most ZINC/YELLOW drywall and chipboard screws are in this category.
Class 2	For general internal use where significant levels of condensation occur. Electroplated ZINC/YELLOW is generally used to meet this class.
Class 3	For general external use in mild industrial and marine applications. The class is intended for roofing and cladding screws in mild applications.
Class 4	For external use in marine and moderately severe corrosive environments, generally within 1 kilometre from marine surf, although topography and /or strong prevailing winds may extend this distance.

Table 6. Different classes of screws.[35]

Should you decide you are aiming for 50 years there seems little choice in the fasteners. They must be stainless (grade 304 or 316) as it is a simple matter of install and forget. Issues of corrosion in zinc screws are well enough known to discount them immediately irrespective of the class they are given but why not galvanized or any Class 4 screw? One reputable manufacturer does say that their screws are suitable for 50 years in a light industrial/urban application which most batten installations will be.[36] There are two reasons for not using them:

---

[32] "Experience has shown that timber with a sawn upper face provides greater long term weathering ability than a dressed surface" Timber Queensland. *Technical Data Sheet 7, Timber Decks – Commercial, Industrial and Marine.* . (Brisbane: Self Published, 2014).

[33] http://www.buildex.com.au/corrosion_management.html. Date accessed. June 7, 2015.

[34] As one manufacturer summed up the present situation, it is down to how much you trust the manufacturer's warranty.

[35] http://www.buildex.com.au/corrosion_management.html. Date accessed. June 7, 2015.

[36] http://www.buildex.com.au/climaseal4.html. Date accessed. June 7, 2015.

- The need for maintenance. The manufacturer that gives the 50 year industrial/urban life has a requirement "that areas not exposed to rain should be washed down regularly. . . . Washing should be carried out at least every six months and more frequently in coastal areas and areas of heavy industrial fallout"[37]
- Whatever you specify has the danger of being substituted with a lower priced and thence the likelihood of a lower performing product.

The question has been raised about the reaction between two dissimilar materials and so should stainless screws be used on a galvanized frame? There is very minimal corrosion with large areas of galvanised (as you would have in a frame) and stainless screws. There is significant corrosion when there is a large section of stainless and a galvanised screw.[38] There can be a problem when using class 4 self drilling screws to attach the batten through a non-drilled galvanized frame as the less well corrosion protected shaft and black steel of the frame, and the swarf created through drilling, are in contact. Rust marks also can occur as a result of this practice. The steel supports should be predrilled prior to galvanizing to avoid this.

Bolts, unlike screws, are not a performance based product. In my book, *Deck and Boardwalk Design Essentials* I write about and illustrate the deteriorating performance of imported galvanized bolts. For this reason I urge designers to specify stainless bolts.

Other Matters
Mounting Horizontal Battens

The pH of various timbers was listed in Table Three where some species are shown as a three and some as a two. The significance of these figures is shown in Table Seven. All Australian hardwoods are acidic, some more so than others. Spotted gum, an ideal species for battens, has a pH range of 4.6 to 5 which is outside of the problem range of 4.3 or lower while grey gum, again highly durable, is more acidic at 3.8 and can have increased rates of corrosion.[40]

Acidity Class	Representative pH value	Boundary pH value
1	5.5	5.0
2	4.5	4.0
3	3.5	

Table 7. Natural acidity classification and representative pH values.[39]

This affects both the choice of fastener (another good reason for using stainless) and the method of corrosion resistance of the frame.

---

[37] http://www.buildex.com.au/buildex_warranty.html. Date accessed. June 7, 2015.

[38] Collinson, Dave. Technical Manager, Buildex ITW. *Pers. Com.* April 2015.

[39] Nguyen, Minh N, Robert H. Leicester, and Chi-hsiang Wang. *Embedded Corrosion of Fasteners in Exposed Timber Structures* (Forest and Wood Products Association: Melbourne 2008) 17.

[40] Bootle, Keith R. *Wood in Australia, Second Edition* (North Ryde: McGraw Hill Australia, 2005) 60-1. On this scale a pH of 0 is highly acidic, 7 is neutral and 14 is highly alkaline. The scale is logarithmic with a 10 fold jump between each unit.

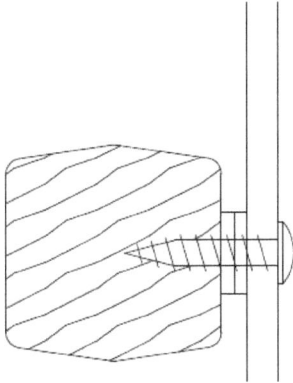

Fig. 26. Separating batten from frame.

It is important that the amount of contact between the frame and the batten is minimized. In Figure Twenty-six I have shown a water shedding profile separated from the frame by two washers. Heavy washers are available and custom washers can be punched on demand. A 6 mm washer can easily be welded to the frame prior to galvanizing. An alternative would be to use neoprene washers/blocks. The horizontal screw, coupled with a drainage gap does not allow any moisture to enter the timber and in time cause decay. Corrosion is also minimized as the timber dries quickly as no moisture is trapped.

Aligning square timber on the diagonal has been recommended as the option that will give the longest life. Figure Twenty-seven shows a suggested mounting detail for the batten. To minimize the contact area you may chose not to use a short length of angle iron but have a custom piece of flat laser cut and bent. This will allow for a sizable hole to be incorporated into the base to shed any moisture. Alternatively, you could incorporate spacers.

The mounting frames seen in Figures Nineteen and Twenty are from standard steel profiles, with Figure Nineteen being a split universal beam. Modern manufacturing processes give you almost unlimited scope in your options. Steel can be laser cut and folded almost as needed.[41] This gives you far more freedom in what your support frame looks like.

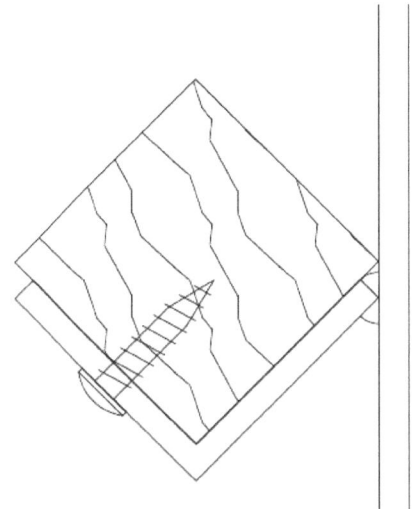

Fig. 27. Aligning on the diagonal

Safety in design

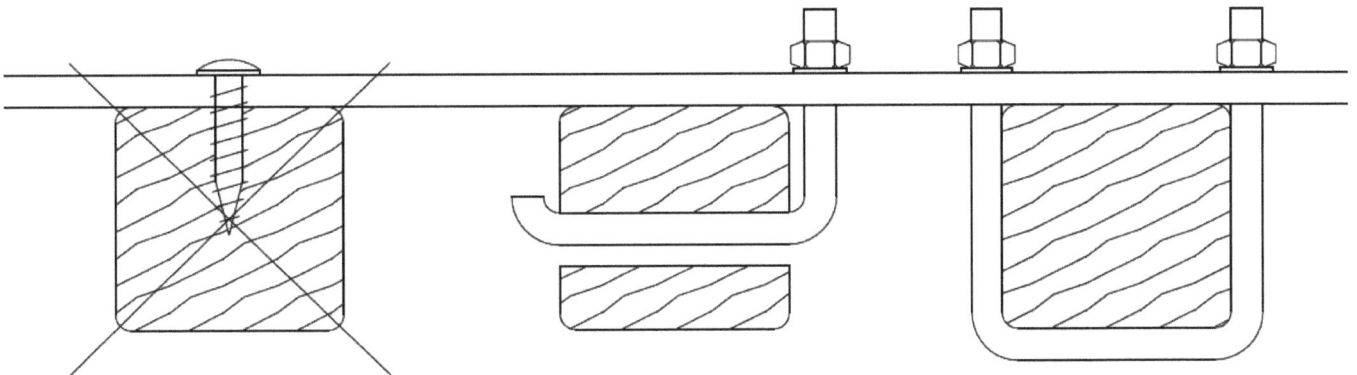

Fig. 28. Suspending battens from under the support.

Mention was made in the Introduction of a project where timber battens were replaced with aluminium. In this case, the timber was suspended from under the horizontal steel frame. The recycled battens were screwed from the top into the back, so hiding the fastener - refer the left hand example in

---

[41] Check the limitations in your market. An example of capability in the Brisbane marker is Bend-Worx at Wacol which can fold 10 mm 316 stainless in lengths up to 8.2m long. You need to allow 72 mm on one side.

Figure Twenty-eight. Moisture was able to penetrate into the screw holes and decay eventuated.[42] After approximately ten years one of the battens fell. The same project also has battens fitted to the top of horizontal supports in other areas. These are faring well and, I hate to state the obvious, but they cannot fall off. In my opinion, the battens suspended from underneath looked more attractive and that was obviously the architects opinion which was why he did it. The centre option in Figure Twenty-Six results in an effect close to that of screwing from the top.

We all have 20/20 hindsight when looking at projects that have not been as successful as was intended. It is so often the case that a stunning piece of creativity can be spoiled by such a small detail. The batten could have also been attached using the method in the centre or right hand of Figure Twenty-eight. It is not as neat as the alternative concealed fixing but it is a set and forget system when lock nuts are used.

In all design work there is the need to stand back, take off the creativity hat and replace it with that of a pessimist and ask, "What can go wrong". A wise man described a pessimist as an optimist with experience. With timber design you can never underestimate the value of experience.

Overhang

The overhang at the ends needs to be considered. If we were referring to boardwalks, not batten screens, you would notice the movement in the unrestrained edges of decking if there is 200 mm overhang. We only go this far in our structures if the edge is covered by a kerb to hide it. When installed high, the visual effect of movement is more forgiving but 200 mm still seems to me to be a good distance to aim for as your maximum overhang. Again, there are no textbooks to refer to give a definite answer and heavier sections are more forgiving.

Galvanised or Stainless Frames?

Laser cutting has been mentioned already. Lasers have come a long way from the scene in the movie Goldfinger where James Bond is about to be cut in two with a very exotic looking but very slow beam. Their availability is now widespread and components cut from them are very cost effective. It is realistic now to have the frame fully cut, with all holes pre-formed. This is all done with an accuracy of 0.5 mm for sheet thickness up to 10 mm. It does not matter if it is black steel or stainless that is being cut. This flexibility means that stainless can now be a viable option[43]. The common sizes in Australia in grade

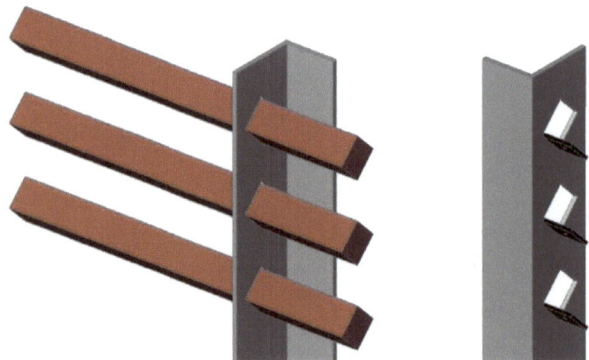

Fig. 29. Possible mounting configuration using laser cutting.

316 are 1500x3000 mm, 2000x4000 mm, 1500x6000 mm and 2000x6000 mm. At the time of writing the biggest laser in Brisbane will only cut 4000 mm long but 6000 mm is available from Sydney.

---

[42] Reference has been made to the recycled standard. The problem could have been exacerbated by the timber as well. I remain amazed how grey ironbark which makes up only 4.5% of the Queensland state forest production can be sold in great quantities as recycled timber.

[43] Our own practice is to use stainless instead of galvanised for our brackets as the logistics are far simpler. We save transport to the galvaniser. The truck may have to wait for hours in a queue to be unloaded, then have several days delay while the product is galvanised and queue again for hours to loaded.

If stainless is chosen, should it then be polished? If you would have been content with a galvanised finish then there is little point providing there are no environmental considerations such as salt air or pollution. You need to consider if reflected light will also be an issue. A 2B finish is available in the thicker sizes that will be required. This finish is suitable for use "in some architectural applications that will not be closely examined for uniformity of finish such as downpipes and gutters".[44] Polishing does, however, reduce the possibility of tea staining.

Frame Fasteners

Just like the support systems, designers are no longer restricted to off the shelf fasteners. With CNC lathes being readily available, it is possible and even relatively economical to design your own if standard product is not ideal.

The grade frequently chosen in stainless is SAF2205[45] which has high mechanical strength, roughly twice that of austentic stainless steel. You will just have to purchase a full bar which is available in lengths from 4 to 6 metres long and in diameters up to 150 mm. Forming Allan key heads is not difficult.

Fig. 30. Custom made 16 mm fastener.

---

[44] Australian Stainless Steel Development Association. *2B, 2D and BA Cold Rolled Finishes.* URL http://www.assda.asn.au/technical-info/surface-finishes/2b-2d-and-ba-cold-rolled-finishes. Date accessed. June 12, 2015.

[45] This is a Sandvik code but is well recognized in the industry. Sandvik say of this duplex stainless steel that it is "characterized by high resistance to stress corrosion cracking (SCC), pitting, crevice and general corrosion and very high mechanical strength." URL: http://www.smt.sandvik.com/en-au/products/trademarks/sandvik-saf-2205/ Date accessed. June 24, 2015.

5. LEACHING AND FINISHES

Weather exposure leads to premature degradation of the timber surfaces, whether it is through UV effects or water absorption. Checking, cracking, delaminating, discoloration, twisting and bowing can be minimised by caring for your battens. Timber coatings do not necessarily improve the timber's resistance to decay and can, in fact, increase the risk substantially as they can reduce the ability of the timber to dry out. On the other hand, they minimise weathering and the potential for fungal organisms to develop on the surface if there is any moisture. A structure such as a boardwalk will give a long service life without any finishes. However, the end section of the members are much larger than we would normally use for an architectural batten. It is important to consider whether a coating system should be used and its ongoing maintenance. But before discussing coatings, the related matter of leaching must be considered.

Leaching of Tannins

The issue of tannin bleed has to be considered in your design. All Australian hardwoods leach tannins, as also do imported rainforest timbers. Some species, like kwila/merbau and blackbutt produce large amounts of extractives while on the other end of the scale, spotted gum probably produces the least. This is another good reason for choosing this species. Figure Thirty-one shows some kiln dried screening I supplied to a project in Japan when I was a novice at producing specialized timbers. The architect thought that if the timber was dry there would be no leaching and I did not know any better at that time. I soon learnt otherwise as the

Fig. 31. And then it rained! Spotted gum battens in Japan.

first time it rained tannin stains ran down the white stonework.

Fig. 32. Blackbutt leaching onto concrete.

Even when the timber is "sealed" tannin can still be an issue. Three coats of a high quality decking oil will not prevent leaching, even on spotted gum. Oiling unseasoned timber, which anything above 50 mm has to be, is not as successful as would be hoped. The oil simply cannot penetrate when the timber is still filled with moisture. Film finishes can even degrade from the inside out due to the effect of the extractives.[46] One manufacturer requires a four to six week weathering period prior to applying their coating or having the timber pre-leached.[47] By leaving an extended period of time between installation and finishing, you would expect to have a problem from leaching if it rains over this period and it makes sealing all around impossible in some applications. Best practice in sealing requires the timber be

[46] Damien McTague, Woodmans Timber Finishes. *Pers. Com.* April 19, 2001.

[47] Intergrain. *Dimension 4 Ultra Primer*. URL: http://www.intergrain.com.au/consumer/products/exterior/product-details/2744. Date accessed. June 15.

coated all around, not just the visible face.

Fig. 33. Pre-leaching timber.

Specifying recycled timber **does not prevent leaching**. The timber may have been in service for 100 years but, as it is normally cut from larger sections such as girders, it will behave exactly the same as green off saw timber. It will generally not be seasoned[48] and will leach in the same way. One way of dealing with leaching is to ensure the tannins drip onto gardens or grass where it will not matter. Another way is to pre-leach using proprietary products and these can be very effective. It does not totally remove the possibility of leaching but it does make it more manageable. When timber has been pre-leached it is more able to receive penetrating oils. The oxalic acid based proprietary products used to leach timber will also effectively remove tannin stains from concrete.

Paint

The use of paint should not be discounted as a finish. It is not just a cheap alternative to using painted steel or aluminium. As one architect observed, "it still has a very timber look ,. . . [and] always looks different to fibre cement or metal".[49] Paint is a very reasonable choice of finishes especially now that we can see manufacturers warranting their product for unheard of lengths of time. One manufacturer warrants the paint for as long as you live in the house while another mentions 100 seasons.

What is causing the change in paint? As one paint chemist said, "They are finally pulling their head out of the sand regarding the variability of timber".[50] Considering the difficulties with timber, the following all impact on the success:

- high to low amounts of extractives,
- high to low pH,
- high to low shrinkage on unseasoned timber (13 to 3 %)
- continual dimension change with moisture content change,

Fig. 34. Painted battens. **Designer:** James Pierce, **Material:** Spotted gum

---

[48] Refer to the project Tree of Knowledge.
[49] Mainwaring, John. *Pers. Com.* April 27, 2015
[50] My source would rather not be named.

- surface finishes from rough to smooth,
- high to low densities,
- backsawn or quartersawn,
- great variability in absorption and
- great variability in grain characteristics.

The wonder is that paint succeeds at all with the stresses this variability can impose!

Generally, you cannot go wrong if you follow the manufacturer's recommendations but I am not so sure that is always the case with paint. Let me explain. Some time ago, I built a truss bridge with painted 50x38 mm balustrades, I had the local sheltered workshop paint them and we used a premium acrylic gloss over a water based primer as was instructed on the can. We left them on a rack for a few days and then stacked them to return to our site. They all glued together and when separated, tore off paint. I called the representative of that paint company and he said that I used the wrong primer. Notwithstanding what was written on the can, I should have used an oil based primer. So much for labels. Even now we could be excused for being a little confused when determining the correct primer as different manufacturers specify differently. In Table Seven, I give in summary form the recommendations of four different paint manufacturers for primers on external acrylic paint.

Dulux Weathershield Gloss	Wattyl Solagard Ultra Premium Low sheen	Taubmans Sunproof Exterior	Accent Solarmax
Self priming on timber[51]	"If painting with white & white tone colours on a tannin rich timber, apply an initial coat of Solagard® as a sealer"[52]	"Tannin rich timbers should be primed with Taubmans Prep Right Wood Primer or Taubmans 3 in 1."[53]	"Where a primer is not specified apply three coats to previously unpainted surfaces"[54]
Table 7. Different priming instructions for acrylic paints.			

My unfortunate experience with gluing from block stacking, though reduced next time around, was not solved by changing to an oil based primer. (The issue was block stacking, not primers, and is something you need to consider if you are specifying a painted finish). The flexibility and permeability of the paint needed to withstand the variability of paint is exactly the reason the timber glued together. But what is the right primer, water, oil or no primer at all? Regardless of the recommendations above, all these manufacturers manufacture a primer suitable for these paints and what are we to make of a comment suggesting a primer may be specified?

A primer is used to provide a strong bond between the wood and succeeding coats. It functions as a sealer and a water repellant, sometimes with fungicides added and is formulated to have a dull finish and so aid with the adhesion of the top coats. When we first started selling paint, the sales representative told us, "Oil and water do not mix, so do not use an oil primer under a water based top coat". It sounds logical but it was incorrect as oil based primers are frequently used under water based paints. Timber Queensland are more specific in their advice relating to cladding which is similar to battens in the terms of risk. They say, "For all cladding where a painted finish is required, boards **should** (emphasis mine)

[51] Dulux. *Dulux Weathershield Gloss Datasheet.* URL http://www.duspec.com.au/duspec/file/AUDD0054.pdf. Date accessed. June 16, 2015.

[52] Wattyl. *Wattyl Solagard Ultra Premium Low Sheen. Data Sheet.* URL http://www.wattyl.com.au/export/download/product_datasheet/D4.14_-_Solagard_Low_Sheen.pdf?pdf. Date accessed. July 16, 2015.

[53] Taubmans. *Sunproof.* URL. http://www.taubmans.com.au/Paints/Sun-Proof. Date accessed. June 16, 2015.

[54] The instructions on the Accents Solarmax can. Date viewed July 17, 2015

be **primed all round** (emphasis mine) with a solvent (oil) based primer plus one coat of undercoat, colour matched to the final finishing coat. This will ensure that significant colour variations will not be apparent due to any shrinkage or movement that may occur later. Knots may be sealed with a two pack polyurethane or other sealer recommended by the paint manufacturer".[55] A primer, most likely oil based, should be part of your paint specification.

What type of paint should you use? In 2006 Timber Queensland advised, "Solvent borne (alkyd or oil) finishes are more resistant to water vapour than water borne (acrylic) finishes. Where a high level of protection is required, a finish system with a solvent borne primer and/or undercoat should be selected". While acknowledging the easier application and the improvements in water based paints, the objection was that "softer films tend to retain more dirt than alkyd (solvent based) paints, and thus harbour more mould growth".[56] Despite advances in paint technology, they saw no reason to revise that recommendation in the March 2014 review of their recommendations. Against this there are now water based enamels that are promising, at least through accelerated weathering trials, to match the performance of the premium acrylics. There can be no substitute for obtaining a written recommendations for a primer and top coat from reputable suppliers especially when new formulations are being released.

A successful[57] painted batten project will include the following:

- a light colour will be chosen to extend the life of the paint and timber,
- there will be no housed joints,
- the ends will be sealed,
- the primer will be checked for adhesion if factory applied and
- the top coat will be applied by brush.

Clear Film finishes

More care needs to be taken when considering whether to use a clear finish on architectural battens than any other alternative. These films can easily be the "maintenance nightmare" that has been referred to earlier. Many professionals have reported very disappointing results to me and a reluctance to use them. This is something I have also observed in many projects and experienced first hand. Film finishes have to deal with the same variability (as mentioned under the *Paint* section above) which cause many of the problems but not all.

Fig. 35. Project finished with clear film finish.

---

[55] Timber Queensland *Technical Datasheet 5, Cypress and Hardwood Cladding*. (Brisbane: Self Published, 2014), 1. Bootle is less definitive with the term "often used". *Wood ...*, 151.

[56] Timber Queensland. *Technical Datasheet 2, Finishes for Exterior Timber*. (Brisbane: Self Published, 2014), 1.

[57] One of my proof readers asked me to share his experience of problems associated with painting with the hope that closer attention will be given to painting specifications generally. He had specified LVL rafters which extended past the house which were coated with a waterbased paint. They were to have a glass roof over them protecting them from the elements. Unknown to him the client deleted this covering as funds were short and as a consequence the LVL's "wet rotted" under the paint. The paint manufacturer replied that some water based paints were "pervious" i.e. that they let water through to the timber and trapping it and not letting the water escape.

UV Blockers are a critical component of clear film finishes. The finish should contain blockers that protect the timber and different blockers that protect the film itself. These blockers are expensive and some low priced finishes have neither! Without the blockers that protect the timber, the fibres start to break down into a fine powder, indiscernible to the naked eye. Once this happens you have a member that is, in effect, wrapped in cling film. The microclimate between the wood and the film can then hasten decay. Any break in the film, which can be caused by natural feature (Refer Figure Thirty-seven), unsealed butt joints, or fasteners can also allow moisture to enter and promote decay. As mentioned under the Leaching section above, the extractives themselves can cause the film to breakdown from the inside out with hardwoods which is why most clear finish manufacturers recommend a leaching period of something like six to eight weeks. But remember, in our drought prone land, if it has not rained, which it might well not have done over an eight week period, it has not leached so you may have to introduce washing as part of the coating plan. Do not expect recycled timber to be pre-leached. The finish should also be of a thick consistency so forcing the painter to put on a heavy coat.[58]

Fig. 36. CN oil on deck and clear film on battens.

Fig. 37. Decay in spotted gum under a premium film finish after eighteen months.

Fig. 38. Film finish on battens.[59] **Project:** Lockyer Valley Sports and Aquatic Centre **Architect:** Fulton Trotter **Material:** Spotted Gum

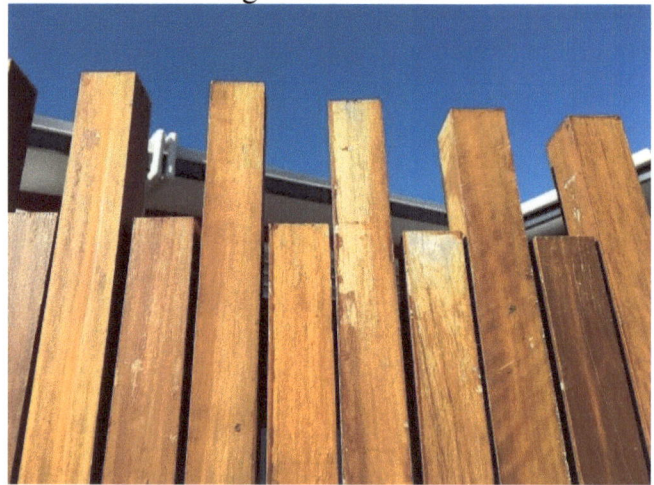

Fig. 39. Film breaking down after six months

---

[58] I am aware of one project in north Queensland where the painter applied three thin coats and after an expensive claim the manufacturer reformulated the finish so it could not be applied thinly.

[59] This fence is a good example of the use of sawmill recovery sizes.

The Achilles heel of film finishes is maintenance. If the film is left to deteriorate it will need to be completely sanded back to bare timber between coats. This means that frequently (if not eventually mostly) recoating simply isn't done. If it is recoated, and it will need to be done on a very regular basis, it will be a costly exercise. The case history of the University of Queensland, Student Activity Centre shows a situation where a film finish is a reasonable option. The building is low, i.e. easily accessible, and the film is sheltered from UV by trees. There will be maintenance but it will be manageable. The 46 kilometres of battens on Lang Park which are up to five stories above ground would be impossible to maintain at an economic price. Film finishes are suitable for internal battens though.

These finishes can be used over rough sawn timber but it is necessary to sand before the first coat otherwise a very rough finish results. Manufacturer's recommendations can include a further sand between subsequent coats. Under no circumstances use steel wool to sand as rust marks can develop on the timber.

Penetrating Oils

There is little doubt that the most robust penetrating oil that can be applied is CN oil (refer the decking in Figure Thirty-six which is coated in CN Oil).[60] The abbreviation CN stands for copper napthenate. Against this superior performance is the unavoidable fact that when it is first applied it looks horrendous. I described it to my customers as having the appearance as if someone has dropped the oil from the car sump over the timber. The smell is not very inviting either. On the positive side the smell quickly goes and the CN oil changes colour to the more mellow and even attractive golden brown we see in the image. Another positive is that it contains a preservative suitable for a seven year period prior to re-application. If there is a possibility it can be used it should be considered. Re-application is not always practical, particularly if there are waterways or pools nearby and other oils may have to be considered.[61]

As for any oil other than CN, if you are hoping for it to work as a preservative, I am afraid the "horse has already bolted". If you have not received the correct natural durability nor treated the sapwood correctly you cannot make everything well by using an oil, even an

Fig. 40. Freshly applied penetrating oil. **Architect:** Ralph Bailey. **Material**: Iron bark.

---

[60] CN oil (or similar and I do not know of a similar) is the product recommended for architectural battens by Colin MacKenzie, Technical Consultant, Timber Queensland. *Pers. Com.* April 24, 2015.

[61] It was this inability to reapply in waterways that prompted us to work with Lonza to develop Tanacoat. Some oils at the time contained some very unsuitable additives for use over water.

expensive one. At the time of writing there are no oils other than CN that can be claimed to be a preservative.[62] The main things you can expect from a penetrating oil is that it **works as a water repellant and a UV blocker**. The same thing can be said about UV blockers in oils as with clear finishes. They are expensive and some products can have very little of them, indeed they can have very little water repellency as well. Fortunately, unlike paint and clear films, penetrating oils are not affected by dimensional change.[63]

People confuse penetrating oil with film finish as, when the oils are first applied, it does have some level of gloss finish but this is frequently short-lived, especially on unseasoned timber. That does not mean it is not present and not working. Throw water on the surface and you could well find that it is still repelling water. Once the surface stops repelling moisture it is time to re-apply. You do not have to sand back at all, simply wash off any dust and kill any mould if present and then re-apply. This simplicity and relatively low cost makes maintenance a possibility. In many situations, reapplication is not practical and all you can hope for is to apply two or three coats prior to installation and from thereafter let the timber weather to silver grey.

How can you tell a good penetrating oil from one that is less so? Glossy cans and brochures and a high price are not necessarily a reliable guide and marketing claims should not be accepted on face value. Technical data sheets also don't necessarily show the relevant information required to determine a "good quality" product, the saying "oils ain't oils" stands true. A good quality oil should contain ingredients like:

- Resin system or oil suitable for timber. Often resins are modified to have characteristics which address limitations of natural oils. This can include mould growth in linseed oil and lanolin.
- UV absorbers which offer protection to timber substrate and resin/oil system.
- Water repellents. These can vary significantly in type and quality. It is good to have something that is not prone to mould e.g. again linseed oil and lanolin.
- Mould and algae inhibitors. These will not remove or prevent mould from pre-infected timber.
- Solvent carrier that aids in penetration of ingredients into timber.

On this last point there are many types of solvent systems. Many penetrating oil formulations contain petroleum based solvents of varying flash points and levels of aromatics as well as those which have surfactants to allow water to be incorporated. The best penetrating oils contain a petroleum based solvent system as it is more able to penetrate into the timber and less prone to facilitate movement of tannins to the surface. A product which incorporates a solvent with a high flashpoint and low aromatics would be preferable. What does this mean? A high flashpoint (>60.5 degC) will mean the product will not be considered flammable thus reducing risks for transport, storage and use. A low aromatic solvent will reduce odour and risk often associated with using solvents. While these features do not necessarily add to the quality of a product they do provide benefits which make oil based penetrating oils more amenable to use and hence get the best result in timber.[64]

---

[62] I was responsible for having one brand which was making this claim reported to the APVMA. If you hear anyone making this claim you need to check it with the APVMA.

[63] Bootle. *Wood...*, 146.

[64] All of these points were considered in the development of Tanacoat. When you are considering specifying a penetrating oil you need to ask probing questions of the manufacturer to ensure you are asking for a product that is at least equal.

If you are going to apply multiple coats over time those oils containing copper should be avoided as this will tend to blacken the timber.

There is one other very important thing you should expect from a penetrating oil. While it is not totally relevant to the subject of architectural battens it is included here for completeness in our discussion about penetrating oils. This subject is the ability to seal CCA into the timber and so alleviate any concerns about touching them. Responsible suppliers are not advocating CCA but the principal remains just as true with other preservatives. This, of course, is only an issue with low battens where the treatment can be touched and a designer or owner is unduly concerned. It may also be a consideration if recycled power poles are used as these will be CCA treated. I stress that this is more about perceptions than reality. When the APVMA looked closely at CCA and orchestrated its banning in many applications it did not recommend the removal of existing CCA timber structures, including children's playgrounds, and has issued the following statement on painting:

> "Will painting arsenic treated timber reduce the risk of arsenic leaching to the surface? Information is limited on the possible benefits of painting treated-timber (including existing structures) to reduce possible risks. Some scientific studies indicate that certain penetrating coatings, such as oil-based semi-transparent stains, when used on a regular basis may reduce the potential for CCA exposure. However, there have been some questions raised about the effectiveness of film-forming or non-penetrating stains because of cracking, peeling and flaking. As such, the APVMA cannot provide any definitive advice at this time on whether there are benefits from painting."

Fig. 41. Leaching tests of oiled CCA treated timber.

Fig. 42. touch tests for oiled CCA treated timber.

The observant reader will have noticed that no clear direction is actually given. When Lonza's Tanacoat was developed in conjunction with my former company, Outdoor Structures Australia, we tested its efficacy in sealing CCA and so remove any uncertainty. It was very successful. Because of the wide variation in quality in decking oils you should not accept claims of being able to seal in preservatives without evidence.

Lanolin Based Oils

Lanolin based products are sometimes chosen as they are perceived as being the environmentally friendly answer but, with the wool grease content possibly as low as 10%, and the petroleum based solvents at more than 60%, it is arguable if this is, in fact, the case.[65] It is probably no better or no worse than any other oil in this regard. This is a totally different issue to whether this particular finish works well or not. Again, we can find unsubstantiated claims of preservation from this type of product.[66] There is a long way from protecting the floors of shearing sheds under a roof to fully weather exposed applications.

As briefly mentioned in the previous section, mould growth can be an issue and inhibitors are required to address it.

Painting Steel Supports

Fig. 43. Rust coming through frame after six months.

Fig. 44. Blooming on galvanized and powdercoated steel.

If you choose to paint the steel supports you must be careful in specifying the coating. The purpose of the coating has to be clearly understood as some are purely decorative while others provide the primary and only means of corrosion resistance. Whatever top coat is chosen, as with the timber finishes, it is important to obtain the manufacturers recommendations for preparation and undercoating which must be followed.

Decorative finishes

I built a bridge once where the handrails were specified "galvanized and powdercoated black" which is exactly what I did. It looked wonderful when first built but I soon had a claim from my customer who was upset at the white blooming on the balustrades, refer Figure Forty-four. The application was not far from the sea and I quickly discovered that these situations needed a very expensive specialty

---

[65] Lanoteck. *Lanotec Timber Seal Material Safety Data Sheet*. URL: http://lanotec.liveserver.com.au/wp-content/uploads/2014/04/MSDS-Timber-Seal.pdf. Date accessed. June 22, 2015.

[66] Deck-doc. URL: http://www.deckdoc.com.au/ Date accessed. June 22. 2015. I easily found four other references to Lanolin being a preservative or reducing wood rot. My understanding at the time of writing is that no lanolin producer has had these claims verified.

powdercoated finish. Having learnt a very costly lesson, I would in future seek a written specification from a reputable paint manufacturer as to the best process and product to use in a given location. Powdercoating and other coatings over galvanizing has its own problems and some manufacturers don't recommend it.

Corrosion Resistant Finishes

When we built a truss bridge, the frame is a one piece fully welded construction which is too large to fit in any galvanizing bath. This means that we have to achieve our corrosion resistance through a painted finish. Far from being a second best option, we can achieve corrosion resistance equal to galvanized with a suitable paint, and even better resistance in a marine environment. We have found a two coat epoxy siloxane system[67] excellent for these purposes but even then our practice is to put a sacrificial coating between the timber and the paint. This is because of the extractives and acidity of the timber. Consider how you can touch up the paint as it will get damaged during transit and erection. Consider, also how to maintain the steel during a major refurbishment after many years. Can it recoated in situ.. It must also be able to be repaired with a paintbrush and not sent back to the paint shop as can be the case with powdercoating.

---

[67] As we have been thanked by customers for introducing them to the product we use, I have no hesitation mentioning it here by name. The product we use is PPG's PSX700 which is derived from a paint produced to withstand the marine environment and intense heat of rocket launches at NASA's Cape Canaveral. The two coat system utilises an epoxy zinc rich primer (or other primers if required) for primary anti-corrosive protection, followed by the polysiloxane which also provides anticorrosive qualities as well as very high gloss, and long term colour retention as required for topcoats. This system meets and exceeds the requirements of ISO 12944-6 C5-M High. This system provides corrosion protection to first maintenance of greater than fifteen+ years. When choosing a paint system you should be specifying to ensure performance that matches this product.

6 CASE HISTORIES

Suncorp Stadium, Brisbane

Fig. 49. Lang park (Suncorp Stadium) fascade.

Credits: Architects: Populous + PDT Architects

How do you make a two million cubic metre stadium fit an "adjacent precinct of some of the smallest, oldest and quaintest timber houses in Brisbane" Timber battens were part of the solution. When the new Lang Park stadium was built, it incorporated four very large batten screens suspended from the face of what would otherwise have been, on the outside at least, a plain concrete and steel structure. They have the added functional benefit of shading sunlight and glare from the large glass walls that are also included.

There are about 45,000 metres of Class 1 recycled hardwood mainly drawn from an old naval wharf in Brisbane that was demolished at that time. This should mean a range of durable species were used.

The battens themselves are ex 45x45 mm (refer to footnote relating to the drawing) with tapered top surface going to a 35 mm face. There is also an arris to the leading edge for easy water run-off. Bottom edge was also tapered up as a feature to play on reflected light and give a more interesting appearance.69 This wedge shape also slightly improved the view from the corporate function rooms behind the screen.70 There was also the benefit of balancing the section as profiles that are out of balance tend not to stay straight.

The profile is a combination of milled and dressed finishes and were rough cut approximately three months prior, to gain some degree of moisture equilibrium and allow some of the tannins to drain. Further treatment to address tannin leaching was done by setting up a temporary poly pipe garden type irrigation sprinkler system, strapped to the top of the screen which was turned on several (3) times over a period of a month to saturate

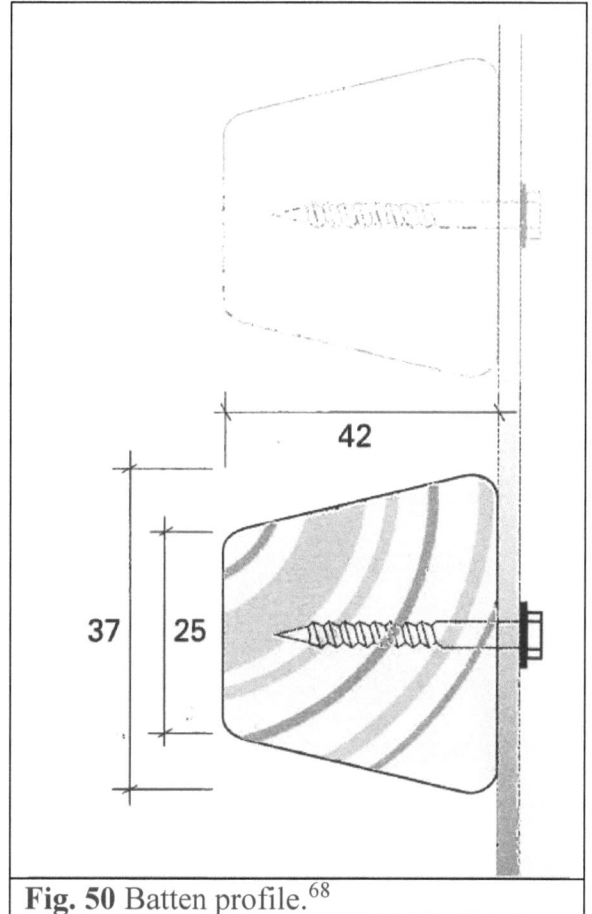

Fig. 50 Batten profile.[68]

the in-situ screen and further leach out as much existing tannin as possible. This was done prior to the finished external paving being installed. It was understood that there would be some tannin staining which was accepted with the understanding it would reduce with age. The slats are fastened from behind with a single stainless steel screw to a galvanized steel frame. This gives a very clean appearance.71 No finishes were applied and the timber was intended to turn the natural grey colour. The galvanized frames were also polyester powder coated (PPC) and were set in approximately 250 mm from battens ends to ensure splitting of timber batten ends was avoided.

David Johnston responded to my questions about whether these battens have been trouble free saying, "The battens have been relatively trouble free, but we would not say completely. As mentioned in your report there are some 45 to 46 kilometres of timber battens (now 12 years old) – of which a minor percentage have required maintenance. This has been due to some natural faults in the timber, and also some instances of moisture being trapped between the back of the batten and the steel support frame. This has occurred more on the screen to the southern façade which does not receive the same

---

[68] David Johnston advised "The batten profile is very close to the profile you found in the *Australian Timber Design* article. A weather shedding profile tapering both top and bottom with pencil round edges to the front. The back of the batten does not have rounded edges as shown in the detail in the article.. The dimensions of the batten in the article do appear a little smaller than detailed. The detailed and specified battens were nominally ex. 45 x 45 tapering down to 35mm at the front. *Pers. Com.*August 10, 2015.

[69] Johnston, David. *Pers. Com.*August 10, 2015.

[70] Johnston, David. *Pers. Com.*August 10, 2015.

[71] Extracted from Timber Research and Development Advisory Council. Origin of timber in *Australian Timber Design Issue 13*. (Brisbane: Self Published, 2003) 30.

amount of sun to dry the timber out".72 I also asked David if there were changes he would make next time around. He replied "Yes – next time around, to avoid the issue of water being trapped between the batten and steel frame, we would include a spacer – as you have suggested in figure 26 of your report."73

---

72 Johnston, David. *Pers. Com.*August 10, 2015.
73 Johnston, David. *Pers. Com.*August 10, 2015.

University of Queensland, Ipswich, Student Activity Centre.

Fig. 51. Activity Centre, University of Queensland, Ipswich Campus.

Credits: Architect: Wilson Architects
　　　　　Project Architect: Phillip Lukin,
　　　　　Builder: Daryl O'Brien, BLOC Constructions.

The Activity Centre, while a standalone building, needed to complement the heritage listed buildings (originally built as an asylum) densely arranged on the ridge at Sandy Gallop, Ipswich.   The site was also landscaped in the Capability Brown tradition. In contrast to the troubled origins of the site, the Activity Centre is a multi-purpose and flexible space set aside for the quiet contemplation and spiritual needs of the students and staff at the University of Queensland, Ipswich campus. The building is close by mature fig trees defining the space and shading the afternoon sun.

The building sits on a polished concrete platform with external walls of recycled timber batten screens combined with fibreglass panelling or louvre galleries. The battens are made from recycled grey ironbark in the sizes 35x35 mm, 40x25 mm and 44x68 mm and clear finished with Intergrain DWD.[74]   "Glazed openings in the screen provide access and frame views. Monolithic interior walls house wash areas, and

Fig. 52. Close up of battens.

---

[74] Riske, Jessica. Practice Manager, Wilson Architects *Pers. Com.* June 12, 2015.

support spaces frame the main prayer space. A canvas blind concealed in the ceiling can be dropped to further divide the space in two. Large doors open up to the fig trees and invert the space, turning it into a stage for community events".[75]

The architect describes the importance of the battens in this way - "Random batten screening sets up a patternless texture to the exterior, punctuated by glazed openings in a glossy counterpoint. The timber warms and humanises the space, inviting touch. It protects and secures the more fragile parts of the building. . . . However the need for privacy is balanced against retaining a sense of connection with the landscape, mediated by the walls. With no eaves for protection, rain and sunlight fall hard against the building. The walls filter light and frame views with deliberate care. Louvres admit breeze while retaining privacy of the users."[76]

This project is a remarkable application of the use of sawmill recovery sizes.

[75]Extracted from Wilson Architects. *Student Activity Centre, UQ Ipswich Campus.* URL. http://www.wilsonarchitects.com.au/student-activity-centre-uq-ipswich-campus. Date accessed. June 12, 2015.
[76] Australian Institute of Architects. *UQ Ipswich Activity Centre.* URL http://dynamic.architecture.com.au/awards_search?option=showaward&entryno=2007040386. Date accessed. June 12, 2015.

Tree of Knowledge, Barcaldine, Queensland

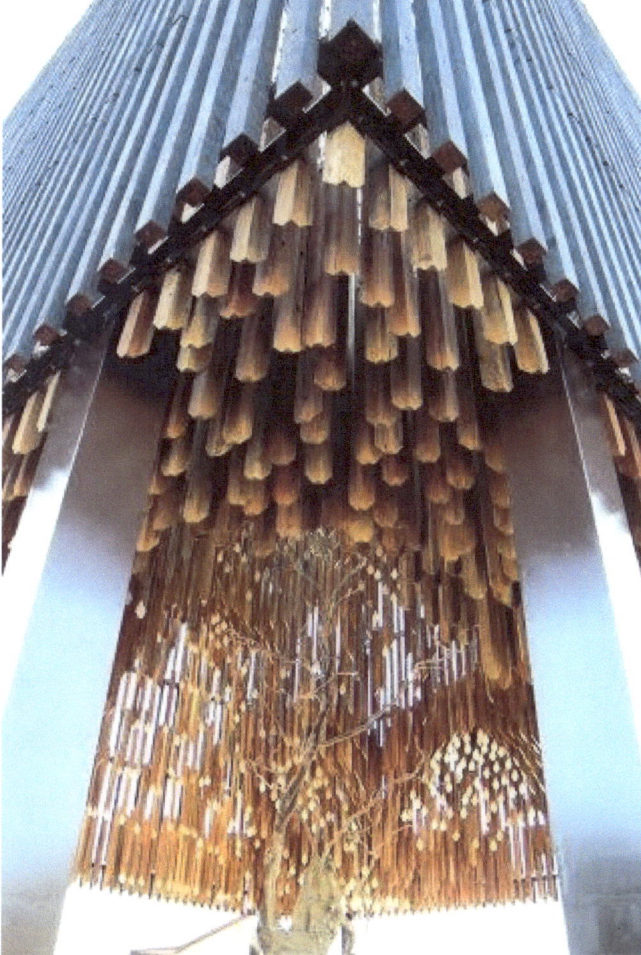

Fig. 53. Tree of Knowledge.

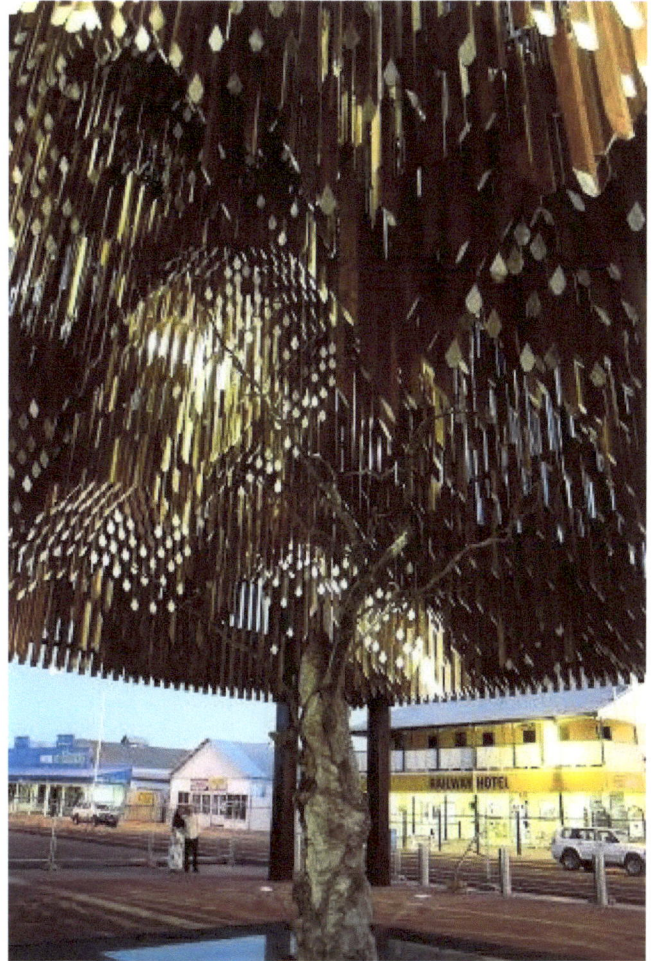

Fig. 54. Tree of Knowledge interior.

Credits: Architect: Brian Hooper Architect & m3architecture (architects in association)
Structural Engineer: Bligh Tanner

Legend has it that the Australian Labor Party was founded by striking shearers under a ghost gum in Barcaldine in western Queensland in 1891. The following year the Manifesto of the Queensland Labour Party was read out at the foot of the same tree. Henry Lawson`s great poem `Freedom on the Wallaby` was also sung here by the shearers with its stirring final verse: "We`ll make the tyrants feel the sting Of those that they would throttle; They needn`t say the fault is ours If blood should stain the wattle."

Unfortunately, in 1991 the tree suffered from dieback which was followed up with political vandalism in 2006 when the tree was poisoned with glyphosate. The remains, seven metres tall and two metres wide, were shipped to Brisbane for preservation. A new memorial was built on the site in 2009 and featured the remains of the original tree. Considering the Tree of Knowledge's very important place in Australia's political history, the construction of the memorial in timber should be noted as significant.

The monument is an 18 m cube clad with 125x125 mm charred recycled hardwood. The "cube shelters and venerates this sacred relic, but also aspires to invoke the living tree as it was in 1891."[77] Inside the cube is a grid of 60 by 60 suspended timbers, again made from 125x125 mm which accurately reproduce the tree as seen in historical photographs. Their alignment is not random. They are placed like "infinitely reflecting mirror cabinets, whether we look up, left or right, we find ourselves pinned at the intersection of insistently receding axes".[78] The sensory effect of being under a tree is enhanced through the play of light and the sound and movement of the suspended timbers. The bevel cut on these members is reminiscent of leaves.

The hardwood hanging members were cut from used telegraph poles. Because the members inside the cube are not rigidly attached but hanging from steel rods,[79] regular inspections are carried out. The timber from this source would be classed as unseasoned for all intents and it would be expected that some would develop major shakes and splits after fixing.[80] Being 125x125 mm it takes years to season even under cover.

Awards:
2009 Grand Prize Australian Timber Design Awards
2009 National Award for Certified Timber
2009 National Award for Public and Commercial Buildings
2010 National Architecture Awards of the Australian Institute of Architects. The Lachlan Macquarie Award for Heritage Architecture and a National Commendation for Public Architecture at the AIA's 2010 National Architecture Awards.

---

[77] ArchitectureAU. *Tree of Knowledge* URL http://architectureau.com/articles/tree-of-knowledge-1/ Date accessed. June 14, 2015

[78] ArchitectureAU. *Tree of Knowledge*.

[79] Hooper, Brian. *Pers. Com.* July 22, 2015.

[80] Refer my comments about the suitability of the recycled standard for smaller sizes. The larger size and perpendicular alignment of the timber would allow for a lowering of quality somewhat.

Gallery of Modern Art - Brisbane

Fig. 55. Gallery of Modern Art (GOMA), Brisbane.

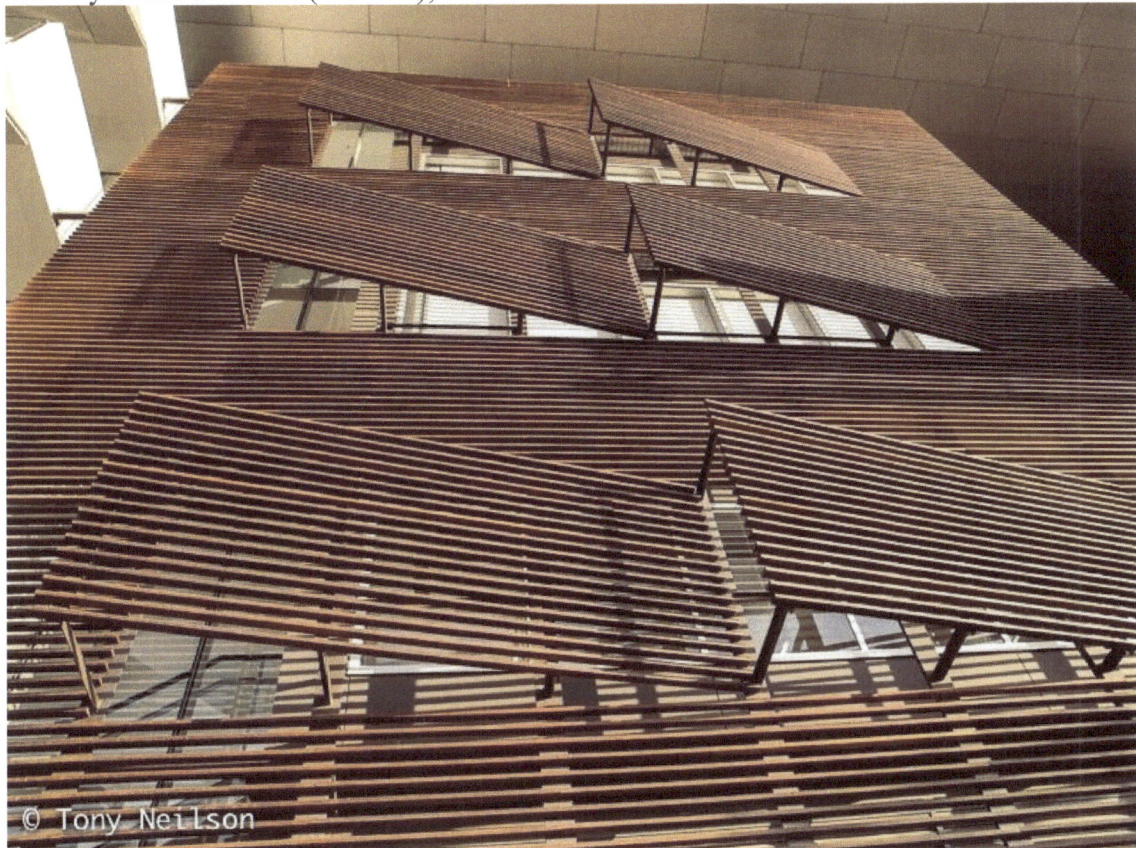

Fig. 56. Gallery of Modern Art (GOMA) Brisbane.

Credits: Architect: Architectus
                              Lindsay & Kerry Clares

The Gallery of Modern Art in Brisbane, known to the locals as GOMA, is situated on Kurilpa Point next to the Queensland Art Gallery and State Library of Queensland and faces the Brisbane River and the CBD, which is just across the river. When opened in 2006 it was the largest gallery of modern and contemporary art in Australia. The Gallery of Modern Art has a total floor area over 25,000 m² and the largest exhibition gallery is 1100 m². Architectus' main design theme is that of a pavilion in the landscape and the gallery functions as both a hub and anchor for this important civic precinct. The building responds sympathetically to the site, its natural topography, existing patterns of urban generation and the river. It has been described as "one of the world's few examples of an architect-designed public art gallery that's really about appreciating the art, rather than usurping it".[81]

Environmentally, the generous roof solves around 90% of the issues facing the Gallery by shading the walls at critical times of the day.[82] Internally, "a restrained palette of concrete, zinc, glass, plasterboard and tallowwood provides a subtle setting for both art and people".[83]

The external battens are a square profile coach screwed from behind to a 150 T steel section, meaning that the edge distance is only about 40-50 mm. The preparation of the timber for the GoMA screen (but given that a film forming coating), there was possibly no leaching of tannins. There is no doubt that the use of battens in this project is very effective but there are also high on-going maintenance cost as Sikkens Cetol is re-applied every 12 months. But importantly, this was not an unfortunate surprise as maintenance has been discussed with client at the design stage and agreed on early in the project delivery.

Compare this approach with that of Lang Park - both projects have their own merits, and both provide very different looking screens.

Awards: 2007 RAIA Brisbane Commendation (QLD)
            2007 RAIA QLD Public Architecture Award
            2007 RAIA National Award for Public Architecture

---

[81] ArchitectureAU. *GOMA*. URL: http://architectureau.com/articles/goma/ Date accessed. June 22, 2015.

[82] Architectus. *Queensland Gallery of Modern art Project Sheet*. URL: http://www.architectus.com.au/sites/default/files/sa-pub-GOMA%202pg%20LR.pdf. Date accessed. June 22, 2015.

[83] Australian Institute of Architects. *Gallery of Modern Art, Queensland*. URL: http://dynamic.architecture.com.au/awards_search?option=showaward&entryno=2007040381. Date accessed. June 22, 2015.

Embassy of the Kingdom of the Netherlands, Canberra

Fig. 57. Embassy of the Netherlands as first built

Fig. 58. Embassy of the Netherlands after the battens have aged.

Credits: Architect: Rudy Uytenhaak (Netherlands)
Philip Leeson (Australia)

The previous Netherlands Embassy building in Canberra was built in 1954 and after sixty years needed to be refurbished and brought up to modern, functional standards. The cost to do this would have been prohibitive and even then the building would not have met the Netherlands government's requirements for sustainability. The Dutch Architect Rudy Uytenhaak in conjunction with Canberra Architect Philip Leeson, was engaged to design a new environmentally sustainable embassy. Rudy maintains that 70% of a building's environmental impact is in its energy use whereas the materials, of which the building is made, by contrast, only account for 30% of its draw on natural resources. He stated the obvious about this building: "If you really lower energy use, you are building something sustainable only if you also lower the impact of the used materials and there embodied energy ."[84] For this reason the building is made relatively lightweight.

The Embassy is designed using Dutch standards for insulation and energy efficient systems which are said to be on an entirely different level to those used in Australia.[85] The timber battens are an important part of the design, being part of the energy efficient design as well as being aesthetic. Rudy advised that "In order to avoid the perpendicular sun load on the east and west façade during morning and evening we shielded the building by a wooden mantle. On the north façade the mantle provides a cantilever. By this orientation and filtering the sun load it is possible to have large windows bringing diffused daylight in to the building. There is no light like daylight, sustainable and vivid. Also the storage of water under and in the pond is used to reflect daylight deep in to the building. Southern light is brought into the central core of the building just behind the roof with PV cells.

The architecture gets its specific character by playing with the proportions of the different parti (elements). I am especially fond on playing with the texture of the materials. So look for instance to the different rhythm in the wooden veil". [86]

The structural designers Royal Haskoning DHV reported that the building uses 70% less energy than comparable buildings and that during a heatwave of over 40 degrees Celsius, it was able to maintain a pleasant environment inside. Much of the heat remains outside because of the insulation, good solar-reflective insulated glass, sun blinds and an optimum position relative to the sun outside. A heat pump also supplies cool air in summer and warm air in winter. The planned outcome was to have a completely energy neutral building.[87] The building is so efficient that, during the heat wave, it was supplying electricity to the grid which was struggling under the drain of air conditioners.[88]

---

[84] Uytenhaak, Rudy. New Dutch Embassy in Canberra: Sustainable and Engaging Interview with the Architect, Rudy Uytenhaak. URL : http://www.uytenhaak.nl/assets/Uploads/Media/Publicaties/HollandFocus03-09.pdf. Date accessed. June 27, 2015
[85] Royal HaskoningDVD *New Dutch Embassy in Canberra Withstands Heat Wave Test*. URL: http://www.royalhaskoningdhv.com/en-gb/news-room/news/20140121-new-dutch-ambassade-canberra-withstands-heat-wave-test/1768. Date accessed. June 27, 2015.
[86] Uytenhaak, Rudy. *Pers. Com.* July 7, 2015.
[87] Kingdom of the Netherlands. *Embassy, Consulate-General and Consulates, Australia, New Chancellery Netherlands Embassy in Canberra 2013*. URL: 2015http://australia.nlembassy.org/news/2013/03/new-embassy.html. Date accessed. June 27, 2015.
[88] Royal. *New ...*

The spotted gum battens are a proprietary modular system by Woodform Architectural. There was no finish applied and they have been left to weather to a silver grey. The wood was intentionally uncoated. The reason for this was explained by Rudy who said:, "Because of the integrity of the material itself, matching with the natural look of aluminium. But also because of the maintenance: as soon as you start finishing products you get the obligation of maintaining that thin layer, covering what you want to expose.

Fig. 59. Concept Click batten system by Woodform used on Netherlands Embassy

In fact, my idea of tectonics in architecture is the possibility to let materials sing. Sing their own song in the orchestra of the materials involved in the building. That's partly about being honest but it's better to speak of integrity. And leaving the material in its natural state, if possible, gets the best aging of the surfaces that border the space. In Holland because of the humid climate there are little woods that can be exposed to our climate. But having seen Australian architecture like the buildings of Glen Murcutt.[89] I asked Phillip Leeson to guide me to the best option for making the natural wooden mantle."[90]

Philip Leeson of Philip Leeson Architects further advised that, "They assisted in the selection of suitable timbers for the exterior of the building and a fixing system which would not rely on screws or nails. We recommended spotted gum for its durability and propensity to grey off evenly. Wherever possible, the battens have been placed vertically to reduce the surface area of timber lying vertically. We have found timber decays faster when it can hold water on the surface and being subjected to freeze/thaw cycles in winter and days of full sun through the summer. We also found a fixing system that used spring loaded clips rather than screws or nails thus avoiding any penetrations into or through the battens."[91]

Awards
2014 ACT Architecture Awards, Light in Architecture Prize.

Author's Note: I have not been able to visit a large project using this system in a harsher environment than Canberra. Specifiers should satisfy themselves of the suitability of this or similar systems in the tropics and sub tropics.

---

[89] Glen Murcutt is an Australian architect that worked alone on smaller projects. This allowed him to design economical buildings that were energy efficient and blended with the environment. Key to his designs was the maxim "Touch this earth gently". This is explored in Philip Drew's book. *Touch this Earth Lightly: Glen Murcutt in his Own Words*. (Potts Point: Duffy and Snellgrove, 2000).

[90] Uytenhaak, Rudy. *Pers. Com*. July 18, 2015

[91] Leeson, Philip. *Pers. Com*. July 21, 2015.

Outdoor Structures Australia's Office

Fig. 45. Outdoor Structures Australia office.

Fig. 46. Walls prepared for battens.   **Fig. 47.** Detail of battens.
Credits: Designer/Engineer James Pierce , James Pierce and Associates.
          Builder: Les Van EE. L&D Constructions.

Working in a small demountable office with three others was a recipe for stress – I had to build a larger modern office. Believing in timber, it did not seem right to do what some in the timber industry do,

Architectural Timber Battens

build in brick and plasterboard! In desperation, I went out and did a stocktake of all my cancelled orders and leftovers from large projects and sent them through to our consulting engineer. He was asked, "Can we build an office from these?". Indeed we could. All I had to purchase was the 100x50 framing and a few rafters. Consulting engineer and not and architect you might reasonably ask. Our consultant has been described as a rare breed, an engineer with an architectural flair. His design was prompted by a building he saw in Austria in 1998 which featured a series of panels of battens hung outside the otherwise concrete building. He also drew inspiration from a pavilion/boat house he saw on the River Lien in Ireland at about that time.

The philosophy behind the use of the horizontal battens was to give the appearance of security as the building is isolated. To achieve this, every second batten extends over the louvre windows (chosen for maximum ventilation) and the front and side doors were covered with heavy timber shutters. In this regard, it was very successful. The only attempts at break-ins were at the back door which was made doubly secure.

The batten is made from Tanalith E treated, kiln dried ex 125x38 spotted gum and ironbark. The board is thicknessed on the worst face and the best face was left rough sawn but was sanded. The top and the bottom were angled to shed moisture. Thicknessing the battens allowed the pencil rounded corners to be formed accurately. The battens were then coated with CN oil and CN emulsion was applied to the ends. They were face fixed with 75 mm 304 stainless batten screws to H3 treated pine battens fixed in turn over 6 mm fibre cement walls.

The internal fit out was predominantly in rose gum and spotted gum VJ. The new workplace was very conducive to harmony and productivity. Not at all a bad outcome considering the constraints of having to work with scrap timber!

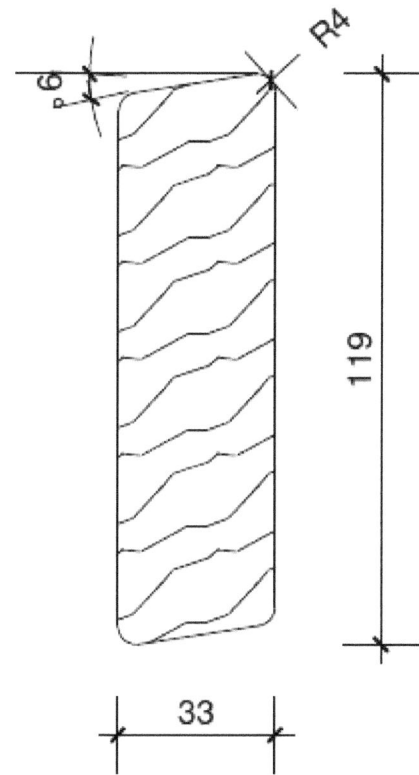

Fig. 48. OSA horizontal batten.

University of Sunshine Coast Library

Fig. 60 Exterior of University of Sunshine Coast Library

Fig. 61. Interior of University of Sunshine Coast Library.

Credits: Architect: John Mainwaring
Lawrence Nield

The University of the Sunshine Coast Library was built in 1997 and, following the tradition of many universities worldwide, it is the central structure of the new emerging university. Libraries by their very nature of having to allocate a large part of their space to storing, acquisition, cataloguing and very individual work areas can be introverted buildings. The challenge was to allow the building to engage with the rest of the university it serves. Critical to this outcome, architect John Mainwaring report that, "The University Building Committee and briefing consultant, Dr David Jones, allowed explorations and interpretations beyond the norm."[92]

What resulted was a library which, while respecting tradition in retaining its central position, also breaks with tradition in the way it opened "out the interior to relate to a surrounding plain and sunny skies"[93] and captures the light and life of the Sunshine Coast. The design of the sun-shaded reading rooms and longitudinal spaces with varying degrees of transparency and translucency was inspired by Louis Kahn's notion of "from silence to light".[94] A grand Queensland veranda[95] sets up the campus axis as a vista and establishes the library as a sociable, flexible focus of student culture.

Unlike the previous projects in this book where the battens were all hardwood, these battens were 40x40 mm select pine which were LOSP treated and then stained to look like spotted gum. LOSP was chosen over a waterborne treatment as it does not colour the timber green (CCA) or brown (Tanalith E or ACQ). The yellow coloured[96] pine allowed the architects to play with light better than the dark hardwoods. John reminisced fondly about that period of his professional life when he said, "For what it is worth, when we were really playing around with the visual effect of shadow patterns, we were having a good time in those days! [it] gets back to that doppler effect, note how the soft light comes through the yellow pine slats compared to if you used aluminum".[97]

There was some decay in the pine reported in 2014 and some sections had to be spliced in. These decay issues were mainly in junctions. From earlier experience with pine battens, John's practice with was to :"isolate and seal the batten fixings with a high quality external flexible mastic to help prevent moisture penetration due to movement due to thermal, rain and corrosion".[98]

---

[92] JMA Architects *Sunshine Coast University Library QLD 1996*. URL: http://www.jma-arch.com/proDetail.asp?proID=3. Date accessed July 24, 2015.

[93] JMA. *Sunshine ...*

[94] "I sense a Threshold: Light to Silence, Silence to Light – an ambiance of inspiration, in which the desire to be, to express, crosses with the possible ... Light to Silence, Silence to Light crosses in the sanctuary of art." Lobell, John. Between Silence and Light: Spirit in the Architecture of Louis I. Kahn. (Boston: Shambhala, 2000) ??.

[95] MacMahon, Bill. *The Architecture of East Australia, An architectural history in 432 individual presentations*. (Stuttgart: Alex Menges, 2001).

[96] Specifiers need to be cautious as now the clear LOSP treatment often has a colour introduced to show the level of treatment. It needs careful specifying to ensure you receive a clear treatment. This product will be more successful in southern states.

[97] Mainwaring, John. *Pers. Com*. July 21, 2015.

[98] Mainwaring, John. *Pers. Com*. April 27, 2015.

Bedales School Art and Design Building

Fig. 62. Badeles school night view.

Fig. 63. Front view showing support system.

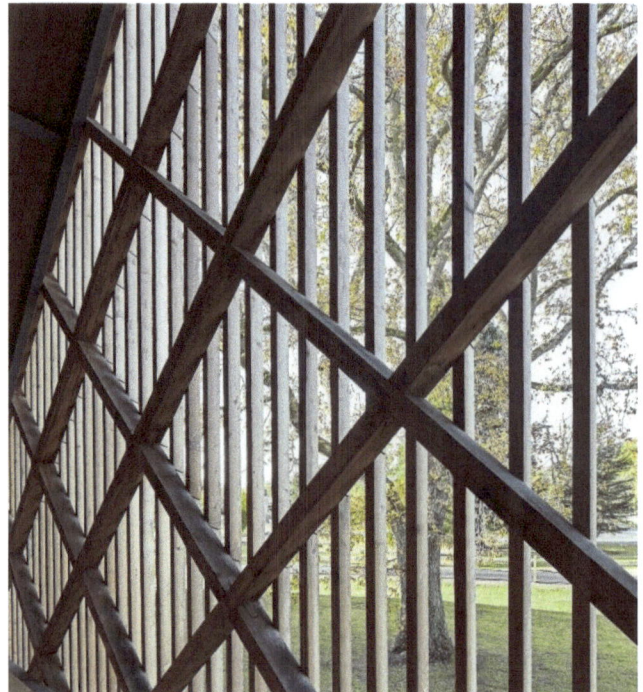

Fig. 64. Back view of support system.

Credits: Project Architect. Tom Jarman, Partner, Feilden Clegg Bradley Studios
Structural engineer, Andrews Newby Partnership[99]

The lattice timber screen illustrated in Figures 62 to 64 creates a welcoming approach to the Bedales School Art and Design Building as well as sheltering the entrance canopy and external walkway. "Larch cladding has been playfully orientated vertically, horizontally, ribbed, laid hit and miss, which all contributes to a diverse range of patterns, shadows and transparencies over the elevations using a single unifying material."[100] Whereas the support system for external battens is generally a "necessary evil" and its visual presence minimized as much as possible, architects Feilden Clegg Bradley Studios, rather, took the frame and made it a stunning a feature in its own right.

The multi award winning Bedales School, (near Petersfield, UK) is set in an area of outstanding natural beauty within the South Downs National Park, in Hampshire. Since its foundation in 1893 the school has had creative arts education at its heart. Because of its location, the school's the new art and design building required a sensitive design, both in style and scale. The chosen arrangement of pitched roof forms refer to a cluster of agricultural barns with clipped gables and sits alongside an existing range of old barns in which 'outdoor work' is taught and students bake bread each week. The arrangement allows the natural rhythm of north light to fill studios on the first floor so reducing the need for artificial light.

The new building, completed in 2016, runs contrary to the ubiquitous 'big box' internalised model employed in many UK school buildings today. By contrast, the designers understood that the connection to the outdoors was a special quality of Bedales life. As a consequence, all circulation is external across covered decks on both sides of the building that double as places to draw, paint, sculpt or just relax and contemplate the environment.. This is enhanced by a large 300 year old oak tree which gives the new building a strong sense of place.

The building utilises a simple steel frame with exposed timber joists to the upper floor roof. Simple materials were used in their natural state throughout. A stable internal temperature is achieved, partially, in this otherwise lightweight construction by the thermal mass of exposed concrete surfaces. Timber-slatted screens and the retained large oak tree both provide solar shading in the summer months. Renewable natural materials, including sustainably sourced timber for cladding and wood fibre acoustic panels, reduce the embodied carbon in the construction. Solar controlled glazing has also been used to windows and roof-lights, varying on orientation to reduce and moderate solar gain.

While the design is extraordinarily effective in its milder (as far as timber is concerned) UK setting, the extreme Australian climate and different agents of attack would require some adjustments. These would include shorter spans on the battens, end gaps and spacing the battens away from the frame.

---

[99] This list is greatly abbreviated. Contact the author for the full credits.

[100] The information in this case history is drawn from information kindly supplied by the architects to the author.

SOURCE OF IMAGES

Copyright of images not acknowledged is held by the author. Copyright of the other images is as listed. All images are used with permission.

Fig.	Subject	Source
Cover		Mark Hogan, Architectus Brisbane
1	Federation House	"(1) Derry(former home of May Gibbs)1" by Sardaka (talk) 08:48, 16 January 2012 (UTC) - Own work. Licensed under CC BY 3.0 via Wikimedia Commons - http://commons.wikimedia.org/wiki/File:(1)_Derry(former_home_of_May_Gibbs)1.jpg#/media/File:(1)_Derry(former_home_of_May_Gibbs)1.jpg
3	Lang Park Stadium	Mark Hogan, Architectus Brisbane
4	Queen Street mall with timber	John Mainwaring, JMA Architects.
6	AIIM Microscopy	Steve Napier, Woodform architectural
7	Netherlands Embassy	Embassy of the Kingdom of the Netherlands, Canberra
8	Tree of Knowledge	"Tree of knowledge monument 1" by Mark Marathon - Own work. Licensed under CC BY-SA 3.0 via Wikimedia Commons - http://commons.wikimedia.org/wiki/File:Tree_of_knowledge_monument_1.jpg#/media/File:Tree_of_knowledge_monument_1.jpg
9	Queensland Industrial Relations Commission interior	Architectus
10	Silvertop ash	Image reproduced with kind permission of www.wodsolutions.com.au
11	Blackbutt	Image reproduced with kind permission of www.wodsolutions.com.au
12	Spotted gum	Image reproduced with kind permission of www.wodsolutions.com.au
13	River red gum	Image reproduced with kind permission of www.wodsolutions.com.au
15	Open cells	Gary Hopewell, DAF
16	Closed cells	Gary Hopewell, DAF
19	Timber join	Mark Hogan, Architectus Brisbane
20	Timber space	Mark Hogan, Architectus Brisbane
25	Boys with pig	State Library of Queensland
30	Custom fastener	Dennis Clark, Dennis Clark Photography
31	Leaching battens	Steve Mitchell
33	Pre-leaching	Nigel Shaw. Wilson Timbers
35	Battens with clear film finish	Tom Lenigas
37	Decay under clear film finish	Nigel Shaw, Wilson Timbers
40	Penetrating oil	Ralph Bailey, Guymer Bailey Architects
49	Lang Park batten	Mark Hogan, Architectus Brisbane
50	Lang Park detail	Timber Queensland
51	UQ Activity centre	Scott Burrows
53	Tree of Knowledge	Brian Hooper, Brian Hooper Architecture
54	Tree of Knowledge	Brian Hooper, Brian Hooper Architecture

	interior	57
55	GOMA outside	Tony Neilson, Neilson Publishing
56	GOMA inside	Tony Neilson, Neilson Publishing
57	Netherlands Embassy, new	Embassy of the Kingdom of the Netherlands, Canberra
58	Netherlands Embassy, aged	Embassy of the Kingdom of the Netherlands, Canberra
59	Batten system	Steve Napier, Woodform architectural
60	USC Exterior	John Mainwaring, JMA Architects
61	USC Interior	John Mainwaring, JMA Architects
62	Bedales School	Hufton and Crow for Feilden Clegg Bradley Studios
63	Bedales School	Hufton and Crow for Feilden Clegg Bradley Studios
64	Bedales School	Hufton and Crow for Feilden Clegg Bradley Studios

REFERENCES

Anonymous. *Dictionary of Timber Terms* (Timber Secretarial Group: Sydney U.D.).

Bootle, Keith R. *Wood in Australia, Types, properties and uses, Second Edition.* (North Ryde: McGraw Hill Australia, 2005).

Davies, Nikolas, Erkki Jokiniemi, *Dictionary of Architecture and Building Construction.* (Oxford: Architectural Press, 2008).

Drew, Philip. *Touch this Earth Lightly: Glen Murcutt in his Own Words.* (Potts Point: Duffy and Snellgrove, 2000).

Kloot, H. The Strength Group and Stress Grade Systems in *CSIRO Forest Products Newsletter No 394* (Sept-Oct 1973). (CSIRO: South Melbourne 1973).

Lobell, John. *Between Silence and Light: Spirit in the Architecture of Louis I. Kahn.* (Boston: Shambhala, 2000).

Road and Traffic Authority. *Timber truss road bridges - A strategic approach to conservation*, (New South Wales Government, July 2011).

MacMahon, Bill. *The Architecture of East Australia, An architectural history in 432 individual presentations.* (Stuttgart: Alex Menges, 2001).

Nguyen, Minh N, Robert H. Leicester, and Chi-hsiang Wang. *Embedded Corrosion of Fasteners in Exposed Timber Structures.* (Forest and Wood Products Association: Melbourne 2008).

Timber Queensland. *Technical Datasheet 2, Finishes for Exterior Timber.* (Brisbane: Self Published, 2014).

Timber Queensland. *Technical Datasheet 5, Cypress and Hardwood Cladding.* . (Brisbane: Self Published, 2014).

Timber Queensland. *Technical Data Sheet 7, Timber Decks – Commercial, Industrial and Marine.* . (Brisbane: Self Published, 2014).

Timber Research and Development Advisory Council. Origin of timber in *Australian Timber Design Issue 13.* (Brisbane: Self Published, 2003).

Woodform Architectural. *Concept Click Batten Screening.* No publication details available.

Websites

Australian Institute of Architects. *UQ Ipswich Activity Centre.* URL: http://dynamic.architecture.com.au/awards_search?option=showaward&entryno=2007040 386. Date accessed. June 12, 2015.

ArchitectureAU. *GOMA.* URL: http://architectureau.com/articles/goma/ Date accessed. June 22, 2015.

Architecture AU. *Into the Cauldron.* URL: http://architectureau.com/articles/into-the-cauldron/ Date accessed. June 12, 2015.

ArchitectureAU. *Tree of Knowledge.* URL: http://architectureau.com/articles/tree-of-knowledge-1/ Date accessed. June 14, 2015.

Architectus. Queensland *Gallery of Modern art Project Sheet.* URL: http://www.architectus.com.au/sites/default/files/sa-pub-GOMA%202pg%20LR.pdf. Date accessed. June 22, 2015.

Australian Stainless Steel Development Association. *2B, 2D and BA Cold Rolled Finishes.* URL: http://www.assda.asn.au/technical-info/surface-finishes/2b-2d-and-ba-cold-rolled-finishes. Date accessed. June 12, 2015.

Deck-doc. URL: http://www.deckdoc.com.au/. Date accessed. June 22, 2015.

Intergrain. *Dimension 4 Ultra Primer.* URL: http://www.intergrain.com.au/consumer/products/exterior/product-details/2744. Date accessed. June 15, 2015.

JMA Architects *Sunshine Coast University Library QLD 1996.* URL: http://www.jma-arch.com/proDetail.asp?proID=3. Date accessed July 24, 2015.

Kingdom of the Netherlands. *Embassy, Consulate-General and Consulates, Australia, New Chancellery Netherlands Embassy in Canberra 2013.* URL: 2015http://australia.nlembassy.org/news/2013/03/new-embassy.html. Date accessed. June 27, 2015.

Lanoteck. *Lanotec Timber Seal Material Safety Data Sheet.* URL: http://lanotec.liveserver.com.au/wp-content/uploads/2014/04/MSDS-Timber-Seal.pdf Date Accessed. June 22, 2015.

Royal HaskoningDVD *New Dutch Embassy in Canberra Withstands Heat wave Test.* URL: http://www.royalhaskoningdhv.com/en-gb/news-room/news/20140121-new-dutch-ambassade-canberra-withstands-heat-wave-test/1768. Date accessed. June 27, 2015.

Sandvik. *Sandvik SAF 2205.* URL; http://www.smt.sandvik.com/en-au/products/trademarks/sandvik-saf-2205/ Date accessed. June 24, 2015.

Uytenhaak, Rudy. *New Dutch Embassy in Canberra: Sustainable and Engaging Interview with the Architect, Rudy Uytenhaak.* URL: http://www.uytenhaak.nl/assets/Uploads/Media/Publicaties/HollandFocus03-09.pdf. Date accessed. June 27, 2015.

Wilson Architects. *Student Activity Centre, UQ Ipswich Campus.* URL: http://www.wilsonarchitects.com.au/student-activity-centre-uq-ipswich-campus Date accessed. June 12, 2015.

ABOUT THE AUTHOR

Ted Stubbersfield was born in the small Queensland town of Gatton in 1950. After studying to be a pastor in Brisbane and the UK he returned to the family business, Gatton Sawmilling Co. A fair question would be, "Can anything good come out of Gatton"? Well, Gatton was the home of a Governor General of Australia (William Vanneck 1938). It is also the home of the best and most innovative hardwood producer in Australia, Outdoor Structures Australia (OSA).

The family had been involved in sawmilling and building for about 140 years and a lot of knowledge has passed through the generations. In 1985 we ventured into the footbridge market (almost by accident) and then followed public landscaping. Initially, we just did as we were told by consultants who knew very little about timber. In about 1988 Ted decided he would come to know the medium he was working with far better than any of his competitors and most of the professionals who used his products.

Ted realised that there were no useful standards and guides for designing and building weather exposed timber structures such as boardwalks. That led in 1997 to his first formal research project on boardwalk design, engineering supply and construction. Over the years there followed a complete set of guides. These allowed professionals to design timber structures of exceptional beauty and durability. Typically, everybody wants to re-invent the wheel and the guides were usually ignored. Invariably, the same mistakes keep being made over and over. This little book is an attempt to remedy this.

In 2012, the time came to close the manufacturing arm of OSA and to take on a less stressful lifestyle. Ted plans to put in writing much of what he has learnt so the industry does not have to relearn it. This book on architectural battens is the seventh in a series of Timber Design Files that are intended to show designers how to avoid the pitfalls of common, but often bad practice as well as Standards that can be very inadequate and engender a false sense of security.

www.ingramcontent.com/pod-product-compliance
Lightning Source LLC
Chambersburg PA
CBHW060813270326
41929CB00002B/28